ISLAND IN THE CITY

AMERICAN LIVES | Series editor: Tobias Wolff

ISLAND
IN THE
CITY

A Memoir | *Micah McCrary*

University of Nebraska Press | Lincoln and London

Library of Congress Control Number: 2017056176

Set in Sabon Next by E. Cuddy.

For Kira, Jordyn, Jarrod, and Kori.

And for my parents. Thank you for
giving me Normal.

We cannot escape our origins, however hard we try, those origins which contain the key—could we but find it—to all that we later become.

JAMES BALDWIN

Love is the difficult realization that something other than oneself is real.

IRIS MURDOCH

CONTENTS

Acknowledgments   xi

NORMAL

Oreo   3

Postures of Privilege   17

To Rebel against Men   26

Ever the Moth   32

CHICAGO

Metropolis   45

Green and Gray   53

Geraldyne's Room   64

Two Cities   73

Playground City   86

PRAGUE

Snow Globe Bohemia   99

Island in the City   106

A Good Fake Czech   116

Cabaret   124

An Idea of Prague   132

Epilogue   144

Works Cited   151

ACKNOWLEDGMENTS

Special thanks go to the following, without whom this project would have been impossible.

Thank you to my Chicago community: my mentor, David Lazar, Mark Augustine, Jenny Boully, Sharon Burns, Alison Carpenter, Warrick L. Carter, Ken Daley, Abby Hagler, Deborah Holdstein, Wes Jamison, Aviya Kushner, Toni Nealie, Colleen O'Connor, Emily Schikora, Ryan Spooner, Jennifer Tatum, Tatiana Uhoch, and Dauren Velez.

To my friends and teachers in Prague: Petr Bílek, Katka Bílková, Morgan Childs, Robin Hemley, Alex Lorenzů, and Hana Zahradníková.

To my community at Ohio University: Ellee Achten, Christine Adams, Aaron Babcock, Jessica Cogar, Piper Daugharty, Alethea Gaarden, David Johnson, Eric LeMay, Jake Little, Sarah Minor, Michelle Pretorius, Tom Tiberio, Elizabeth Tran, and Brian Trude.

Not least of all, many thanks go to the editors of publications in which excerpts of this book have previously appeared (albeit in slightly different form): "Green and Gray" originally appeared in *Midwestern Gothic*, vol. 11, Fall 2013, pp. 59–66; "An Idea of Prague" originally appeared in the online journal *South 85* in Fall/Winter 2016; "Island in the City" originally appeared in the online journal *The Swamp* in Summer 2017; "Metropolis" originally appeared in the online journal *Slag Glass City* in May 2017; "Oreo" originally appeared in the online journal *Identity Theory* in March 2014; "Two Cities" originally appeared in *Midwestern Gothic*, vol. 23, Fall 2016, pp. 18–26.

NORMAL

OREO

"There will be people who'll cross the street to avoid you because you're black," my mother would tell me when I was younger in every conversation or argument we ever had about race.

"Don't be a nigger," my older sister once told me, as she sat with a friend doing sociology homework when she was in high school. I must have been five at the youngest, nine at the oldest. I think I had asked whether she thought I should be wearing a du-rag.

"Nigger," H. G. Bissinger writes in *Friday Night Lights*, a book about a high school football team in a small Texas town: "The word poured out in Odessa as easily as the torrents of rain that ran down the streets after an occasional storm, as common a part of the vernacular as 'ol' boy' or 'bless his 'ittle biddy heart' or 'awl bidness' or 'I sure did enjoy visitin' with you' or 'God dang.'"

Bissinger, having just left an editorial position at the *Philadelphia Inquirer*, decided he would follow alongside Permian High School's Panthers throughout their 1988 season. We learn that the team goes undefeated, eventually losing the state championship. Bissinger gives the book the subtitle *A Town, a Team, and a Dream*.

On "nigger," he later writes:

People who used the word didn't seem troubled by it. They didn't whisper it, or look chagrined after they said it. In their minds it didn't imply anything, didn't indicate they were racist, didn't necessarily mean that they disliked blacks at all. Instead, as several in Odessa explained it, there were actually two races of blacks. There were the hardworking ones who were easy to get along with and didn't try to cut corners and melded in

3

quite nicely. They deserved the title *black*. They deserved the respect of fellow whites.

And then there were the loud ones, the lazy ones, the ones who stole or lived off welfare or spent their whole lives trying to get by without a lick of work, who every time they were challenged to do something claimed that they were the helpless victims of white racism. They didn't deserve to be called black, because they weren't.

Though Bissinger's story takes place in Texas in 1988, I never saw much of a difference growing up in the eighties and nineties between Odessa and my hometown of Normal, Illinois. The word "nigger" wasn't a part of Normal's vernacular, but I could feel, because of the things my family pointed out to me, the difference between "the hardworking ones" and "the lazy ones," "the quiet ones" and "the loud ones," and the way that everyone saw them. I knew my sister and my parents didn't want me to be one of the loud ones. They surely didn't want me to be lazy.

"One of the difficulties about being a Negro writer," James Baldwin writes, "is that the Negro problem is written about so widely. The bookshelves groan under the weight of information, and everyone therefore considers himself informed."

But Baldwin, like my parents, couldn't foresee the change in eras. I cannot know what it's like to fear bombings at my church or be the parent of an Emmett Till. I cannot harbor the exact same fears my parents projected because I am a baby of a post-whatever generation. And while Baldwin acquainted himself with the Negro "problem," he could never see it evolve into an Oreo phenomenon.

In 1969, when my parents met, blacks had been allowed to live in Illinois State University's dorms for only twenty years.

I've asked my mother what it was like to be black, in Normal, in 1969. "Well," she told me, "when you went to the store they followed you around all the time thinking you were gonna steal something. And the police would follow you around. It was hard to get a job, but it was harder for men to get a job than it was women. And they wouldn't want to rent an apartment to a man, but they'd rent one to a woman. But, I mean, overall it wasn't that bad."

I interpret "it wasn't that bad" as meaning it wasn't Mississippi. Wasn't Alabama. It wasn't Texas or even Louisiana, where my grandparents had come from. My mother herself wasn't born and raised in the South; she was born in Waukegan, Illinois, to a family of stragglers from the Great Migration. She moved to Normal to study physical education at ISU. There she met my father. Started a family. Raised four of us in twin cities of 129,000 people. My father was studying political science and communications, but when my oldest sister was born my parents decided not to finish college.

"Most black people at ISU," my mother says, "their major was communications. I think because. . . . Well, for the black men, if you were an athlete you took communications—I don't know if it was because it was easy or not. Almost all of them had communications majors."

"You had to carry a B-average to be a communications major," my father contends. "*I* thought most of them had sociology majors. It was the most popular major for black people. Unwed mothers and stuff. I mean, that's the culture we came from. That's why most of them were sociology majors."

"The culture we came from" being one of unwed mothers stirs a curiosity in me, makes me wonder about my grandparents' generation and the children they bore without present fathers. This is supposed to make sense to me, I think. That black fathers are not present. That they flee.

My mother eventually switched her major from PE to English. She said it was easier, that it required fewer credits to graduate. But after my sister was born it didn't matter anymore, because my mother just needed a job.

My parents met while pursuing their education in a program for blacks and Latinos (then referenced as "Hispanics") called the High Potential Students Program. My mother worked for the program, kept records, and was a typist, and my father was a student.

They met at the same university on whose campus I spent my time growing up, riding my bike and Rollerblading through the quad as I got to know my town on my own throughout junior high and high school. Looking back, I understand it must have been strange for college students to see children on campus while walking from class to class, but this place was a part of *my* town, I thought, and they were only visitors. I had as much right to this campus as they did, reinforced by my love for the environment. I'd fallen for the campus architecture—the music building built like a miniature castle, the enormous five-or-so-story library—and for the professors with their ties and briefcases (so different from my parents, wearing blouses and khakis and sweaters to work), and I know that a part of my development began right there, in an idyllic portrait of my childhood filled with patches of grass and students much older than myself.

This environment more than any other probably formed a worldview for me. Different from my father's Chicago streets and my mother's suburban parks, the college campus was a bubble, a place engineered for surface-level equality. I would learn that the campus wasn't like my junior high school, where too-cheap jeans meant pauperized parentage or where a faction of hip-hop fans, mostly black, sat at one lunch table while another table of students, myself included, talked about rock and Top 40 songs. I first observed a real division in my life in junior high, where two types of black children split themselves up in the lunchroom and I was clearly the type to sit with my white friends. There was no rap music for me, no afterschool basketball. I was accused of being an Oreo.

The education of a black American on how to be a black American begins in the home, then spreads through experience and literature and misfortune and luck. Whether or not it was my parents' intention, my home education left me without a sense of Black Pride and instead instilled only fear. Until my twenties I grew up thinking I didn't want to be black—I just wanted to be a person, someone who could be raceless. As a boy I understood that people were different but couldn't understand why anyone made a big deal of it. I had found it strange, still find it strange the way race can be created simply by recognizing it.

My reluctance comes, I think, from the fact that I *am* black and that I'll always be perceived as black. I can't fight this with anyone, nor would I want to—the visible recognition of myself as a minority is already ever-present, and it would be a futile fight. But I suppose it's also true that I'm an *Oreo*, harnessing a kind of white sentimentality within my black body. When I was younger I used to wonder whether this was how I made friends; because I didn't fit the black stereotype I wondered if the other children fought or shed their own reluctance in befriending me. The children I grew up with were mostly white, a few of them some kind of Asian or Latinx, and only the children of my parents' friends were black. And what of my friends' parents, I wondered: How many of them cared that their daughter or son had a black friend? Why would people cross the street to avoid an identity that wasn't my choice? Would someone sitting next to me on a bus move their seat because I'm black? As a child, was I supposed to cry when someone called me a nigger (or sometimes Micah McNigger)? And if I didn't cry, if I wasn't upset, would that make me a bad black person? What does it mean to be a *good* black person? Is it the same as being a good Russian or a good American, loving vodka or baseball as clear signs of loyalty?

"The American image of the Negro lives also in the Negro's heart; and when he has surrendered to this image life has no other possible reality" (Baldwin).

These questions and more were all I could think about as a child and as a teen, struggling to find *something* to define in myself in a town where the only clear definitions of race looked like a picture of 1988's Odessa, where there were two obvious categories of black people. Had I grown up somewhere other than Normal, or had I grown up poor, perhaps I would have come to understand in a much different manner the ways race and class work. But these things are sometimes subtle to a child—and though I knew how my town viewed and talked about class, I was only just figuring out where to begin with race.

My education in the classroom has been a different story. The most seminal racial texts I can remember encountering are Mark Twain's *The Adventures of Huckleberry Finn* in high school, and both in college and in graduate school James Baldwin's *Notes of a Native Son*.

Baldwin called America a "country devoted to the death of the paradox." Here I am, his paradox, my own American psychology combining the politics, aspirations, and convictions of the whites around me as a child with this black paranoia—a potential riff on W. E. B. Du Bois's "two warring ideals in one dark body." My ideals *have* been at war. Adulthood has had me concede, tipping the king in my childhood and teenage ambitions toward racelessness.

I react, mostly, to Baldwin's essays "Many Thousands Gone" and "The Harlem Ghetto." His critical breakdown of the Negro in America, in contrast to Richard Wright's *Native Son* (in "Many Thousands Gone") and to the New York Jew (in "The Harlem

Ghetto"), helps explain some of the plights lived by those of us in marginalia. But overall the pieces are temporal failures.

"Many Thousands Gone" itself, on the surface, is not a failure, as it was written with all the knowledge one can have of one's own era, however the writing (the first-person plural presumably belonging to the white American) should have essayed to predict from Baldwin's Afro-American-European vantage the possible trajectories of the black American. "He is a social and not a personal or human problem," Baldwin writes, and our goal with social problems should be to anticipate their solutions throughout the hours.

If the black American is a social problem, are people like me the solution? Because we (blacks who rail against stereotype) exist, I wonder if we're looking at the tail end of Baldwin's thesis: "The Negro in America can only acquiesce in the obliteration of his own personality, the distortion and debasement of his own experience, surrendering those forces which reduce the person to anonymity and which make themselves manifest all over the darkening world."

We are not solely talking here about the Educated Black, often seen as outliers in our history and containing the faces of those like Frederick Douglass and Martin Luther King Jr., but rather those more like Will Smith or Bill Cosby, who were trailblazers for what Baldwin seemed not to foresee: a new black whiteness.

In his 2011 *Grantland* article "The Rise of the NBA Nerd," Wesley Morris writes that "21st-century blackness has lost its rigid center, and irony permeates the cultural membrane." Families on television like the Bankses in the nineties' *The Fresh Prince of Bel-Air* and the Huxtables in the earlier *Cosby Show* gave the country a new kind of black American: educated, well-off, and far distanced from any inkling of culture-perceived *niggerness*, from the qualities of the black American we're mostly wary of confronting. Aside from our obvious class differences, these characters were almost everything I wanted to become when I was younger, their erasure from conventional (i.e., stereotypical) blackness a beacon for those of us not fitting in with convention in the first place.

"The Negro in America can only acquiesce in the obliteration of his own personality."

There is nothing in this world that I'm more afraid of being than a man who is testicular, aggressive, and black all at once. In fact all of my performances are the result of a paranoid persona related to both blackness and masculinity, and so my acquiescence isn't as much a way of "passing" in America as it is avoiding a fear of my potential self.

"Black people are unnerving," the video essayist John Bresland writes, "because they're paranoid. They see racism everywhere, even where it isn't." I'd like to raise my hand here, to own up to this paranoia, to worrying out of some infantile fear about where racial prejudice actually exists, even though I believe this prejudice might sometimes be much less about the process of othering than it is a compulsion to love those like ourselves. Isn't hatred, after all, usually in defense of something we love?

And "although the two can be confused," writes the essayist Eula Biss, "our urge to love our own, or those we have come to understand as our own, is, it seems, much more powerful than our urge to segregate ourselves."

But I haven't even loved "my own." Outside of my family I've managed to remain close to no other black people, and I have no excuse aside from my hometown being Normal, Illinois. Which is not to say that this is a real excuse; it's more a reason spurred by my discomfort with the subtleties of race in my hometown.

I can't confess to obliterating anything black about myself, because, growing up, I never saw my blackness in the first place. Race wasn't an issue in day care, where I was the only black child in my class, nor in kindergarten, where I was the only black child yet again.

And I think things remained this way until second grade or so. By the time I met other black children in my classrooms, I had already come to understand that I was different. And that my immediate family was different—that we acted and spoke differently. I remember noting how the other black kids at school sounded when they spoke. I can even remember asking my father once when I was about five how, when I answered the phone, I could tell whether the person on the other end was black. I wish I could remember his answer.

I wonder what Baldwin means when he uses a word as strong as "obliteration." It implies a scale, implies that when there *is* a scale for whiteness it is applied only to minorities and that being *less* black or *less* Asian or *less* Latin means becoming *more* white and not option C or D. To *obliterate* seems as if it should mean getting rid of the -ness altogether, becoming instead something unidentifiable. Baldwin did write, later in "The Harlem Ghetto," that "the American ideal, after all, is that everyone should be as much alike as possible." And that Americanness, rather than blackness or Asianness or whiteness, means anonymity. But perhaps I come up short of understanding. If this is what it means to be an American, it doesn't seem that Baldwin thinks this is a bad thing.

". . . the distortion and debasement of his own experience."

In "The Harlem Ghetto," Baldwin writes, "It is part of the price the Negro pays for his position in this society that, as Richard Wright points out, he is almost always acting. A Negro learns to gauge precisely what reaction the alien person facing him desires, and he produces it with disarming alertness." Baldwin maintains consistency in his theses; he seems to believe, through and through, that the black American can never really be himself if he wishes to get along in the white world, but he shares no specifics of how he should "be himself" as part of a unified blackness. I don't believe that I myself have so much *performed* nonblackness as I have had to learn, from a young age, about the qualities of blackness from family, friends, and other schoolchildren, and then adapt to this learning. These things *are* socially learned, aren't they? We're natural in our actions and expressions until someone guides us in another direction, saying things like *Don't be a nigger* or *Discretion is the better part of valor*.

Once, my younger sister, Morgan, and I were swimming at a Four Seasons and asked my father whether we could stay at the pool longer. I was in the hallway next to my father, and I could see the pool through the window while I pleaded with him to give us more time. He gave me the okay and I rushed through the hallway, through the locker room, and back out onto the pool deck to let Morgan know we could stay. Censoring my excitement and obeying the safety rules, I stopped running once I reached the pool deck. But to make up for this I yelled across the entire pool to Morgan, who was floating in the shallow end and in perfect view of my father. We can stay! Dad says we can stay! Merely seconds later, before I could even jump back in, I saw my father motion with his index finger to come to him, out of the pool, immediately. A cold face said all he needed to say.

After we dried off, dressed, and grabbed our things, we walked out to my father's truck. I was both sad and confused at his apparently mercurial decision-making. He remained silent until we began the drive back, and at this I quivered. I always quivered at his silence. He told us, shortly after the truck left the parking lot, that had I not let the entire pool know our business we would have been able to stay. That I needed to learn discretion.

Now I sometimes notice the looks on people's faces when black children are loud in public. It's a look of sure disapproval, perhaps not toward the children themselves but toward the assumed negligence of the parent(s). Children yell, yes, and they play and scream and laugh gutturally, but it's the heightened volume of children *talking* that gets adults' ears perked. Where did he learn that? Why do they talk about such things?

When a child speaks loudly everyone in range listens, and one can only hope the child has something delightful to say.

The problem with the social decorum of black children playing is that their loudness comes off as a shortcoming—as a thing all right for only nonblack children to display. Adults cringe, *I* cringe, at some of the things these children say, and we probably therefore do degrade the image of this child. (On this point Baldwin and I agree.) Perhaps, in public, this was always on my father's mind; perhaps he was always worried about playground talk of sex or money or the things we saw on television, a clear reflection of his sentiments as a parent.

"...surrendering to those forces which reduce the person to anonymity."

What if I've desired anonymity? What if it wasn't a forced thing? There's much history about the forced anonymity of women and those in LGBTQ communities, while the other side of the coin suggests a *desired* anonymity of Jews, blacks, and those of biracial ethnicity. If Baldwin is right about America's melting-potness, then I want to know more about this desired anonymity.

I want to know more, I think, because as a child and as a teen I never escaped the notion that I could rid myself of my blackness if I worked hard enough at it. I wanted to melt into America's heat through and through, becoming someone who wouldn't be more noticeable than others, even if he *was* a black body in the face of a white background.

Desired anonymity, then, is not necessarily a point of surrender. In October 2011 the *Harvard Crimson* ran Zoe Weinberg's "Raceless Like Me," an article laying out a spectrum for students at Harvard University who wish to push the boundaries of racial identity. At one end, the *raceless*, at the other, the *racially transcendent*, and somewhere in the middle, the *aracial*. The difference is that "racial transcendence," coined by Harvard's Dr. Kerry Ann

Rockquemore, comes off as both lofty and naïve, in danger of being confused with *color-blindness*, which "advocates ignoring race without confronting the inequality and discrimination it breeds. *Color-blindness* implies that racism can be solved passively."

"Racelessness," Weinberg writes, quoting Rockquemore, "is far more complex, because people who transcend race 'are actually aware of how race negatively affects the daily existence of people of color. They have very likely experienced discrimination, yet they respond by understanding those situations as part of a broad societal problem: one in which they are deeply embedded, but not one that leads to their subscription to racial identity.'"

If I see *black* as a description rather than an identity, I believe I spoke aptly earlier when talking about my youthful wish to be raceless. Though *aracial* may be fitting for someone with more than one concretized heritage, *raceless* seems to be the word for those of us making thought-out decisions about our identities. But a potential roadblock here is that I *don't* have more than one concretized heritage: I could speak to you about my French and Irish family names or my Creole great-grandfather, but there's nothing I can grasp the way one can grasp having one black and one white parent. In essence, at the bottom of this issue might be my jealousy toward the bi- and multiracial, as the status quo allows them to check the *raceless* box.

Much was unearthed in the *Crimson*'s interviews with students, ranging from biracial students literally checking the *black* box because they wanted to raise statistical awareness of inequality, to those who check it because "it is so overwhelmingly in your favor to identify by race if you're a minority," as student Anjali R. Itzkowitz stated. "You would be a fool to say you're raceless if you're black."

The boldest question "Raceless Like Me" poses: "If we know race is a social construct, at what point do we begin the process of deconstruction?" This is the kind of question Baldwin didn't ask and should have. My answer, at least at this point, is within our personal relationships. And I'm a hypocrite because, growing up, I let my friends talk about how "white" I was without correcting them—but if I had done things right I would have started with them. Just like talking about our crushes began with them and talks about our parents' money began with them. In my social development and snowballing realizations, everyday talk, not haute scholarship, is where the deconstruction should have begun.

Writing about race as a subject is difficult not because it's hefty but because I have so many biases toward it. I'd very much like *not* to be lumped in with writers considered to have made notable contributions to black and African American literature because I'm not writing about *a* or *the* black experience—I'm not writing *as a* black man. Please remove me from the discourse, because I don't represent anyone but myself.

However, another hurdle of self-representation *within* marginalia is that some readers, inevitably, will feel I represent them as well. It always seems dangerous to write about *othered* groups without fear of *mis*representation, which makes me want to avoid labels even more. What I really want is just a slight inverse of one of Baldwin's own wishes: I want to be a good man and an honest writer.

Being an honest writer means that I cover my bases, that I stick to the facts as I know them and, when necessary, scrutinize the little things. It isn't our job as writers to worry about fact-checking our memories, but there are certainly other things that need to be corroborated: the clinically biographical facts to extract in our writing, the names of streets on which we've lived, the things that, without showing research, would have us admit to laziness. I'm doing my damnedest to be sure I've checked up on the crucial bits of my life.

It's necessary for me to make sense of the ways I've read the world through my experiences and to ensure that as I've moved through life I haven't brushed off the wrong experiences. "An author is not to write all he can," according to John Dryden, "but only all he ought." And I ought, for the sake of my own sanity, to begin evaluating my decisions and my experiences.

One day at recess, Hermann, a boy with a dark mullet who licked his lips beet-red, called me a nigger. It was the first time I had ever been called a nigger. I told on him not because I was hurt or upset, but just because I wanted to see what would happen to him. I enjoyed the eye-widening of the recess supervisor when I told him what had happened, and I knew he'd move quickly to find this boy and bring him to justice.

I don't know nor do I think I ever knew what happened to Hermann that day, as he was dragged away by the arm by one of our lead supervisors near the end of recess. But I discovered power in a word—power that, at seven or eight, I knew I was using the way *he* had wanted to. I had turned his dominance back onto him.

I still wonder about that power. I wonder whether, had I felt less racially neutral, I would've made far different decisions, far different observations. I wonder if, had I felt a little blacker, whatever that might mean, recess would have ended the same way.

POSTURES OF PRIVILEGE

Though I was twelve, I can remember watching Baz Luhrmann's *Romeo + Juliet* for the first time as if it were just days ago. The film starred Leonardo DiCaprio and Claire Danes, neither of whom I'd been aware of before, and it was a flashy and hip film—like a gunfire musical meant to capture the unrestrained spirit of the 1990s.

It captured more than just this for me. Being twelve, I'd had a fair number of on-screen crushes in my life by then, ranging from *The Mickey Mouse Club*'s Annette Funicello to Audrey Hepburn and Aunt Becky (portrayed by Lori Loughlin) on *Full House*, but *Romeo + Juliet* was different because it gave me not one but two screen crushes: I was taken by both Danes and DiCaprio.

I'd known throughout my childhood that I was a queer boy, but I was waiting, I think, for something more dramatic than schoolboy crushes to shake me into myself. I hadn't done that cartoonish gulp—that obvious *Tom and Jerry* gulp that happened whenever a "sexy" cat or mouse walked by—for any male on screen before DiCaprio, and this somehow told me more about myself than any of the crushes I'd had on my male classmates.

I remember that I also used code: I used to say "cool" around my father and other relatives when talking about some of the boys at school, when what I'd meant was "cute." I'd done this since first being thrown into a schoolroom with other children, which was what it took for me to realize what I was. I held onto this code for a long time.

I wonder if the complication here lies in my lack of childhood vocabulary. I didn't know how to articulate what I felt because I

17

didn't know that what I was was even possible. I'd known that there were gay people in the world, and of course that people could also be straight, and this never confused me; I'd never met or heard of anyone who admitted an attraction to more than one gender, though, which made me feel like an even stranger child. I confused myself by thinking I just didn't know what I was *yet*—that I'd grow into it someday, turning out either gay or straight. But when adolescence came around and my eyes kept looking for the same things, I felt pretty resigned to my fate. By then I'd learned the words I needed for my expression, and out of fear I kept them to myself.

Less than a year after I figured out how to articulate my bisexuality, Matthew Shepard was murdered. His death made me begin to think, living in Normal, Illinois—a socially conservative town— that it would be a bad idea to come out, so I kept my orientation a secret from family, and even from the friends I'd spent all of grade school with. After all, I'm black and male, which already felt like two strikes against me. I had no desire to add a third.

Because seventh grade was a time for peacocking, for showing off what we had in order to attract our first dates to school dances, I joined a crowd of straight boys. The thing about straight boys in junior high, though, is that they're not only heterosexual but hyper-heterosexual. I can't count the number of (male) friends on whose bedroom walls I saw posters of supermodels and other attractive female celebrities. A boy had to proclaim his sexuality to find camaraderie in it, a way of saying we were all in this puberty thing together, but the harm in this was that it may have fostered what Adrienne Rich called "compulsory heterosexuality," or the idea that one must perform heterosexuality to perform normalcy.

I kept it a secret that I listened to Christina Aguilera and read issues of *Teen People* and little DiCaprio biographies. I didn't share that I explored DiCaprio's entire filmography and television projects. I wouldn't have cared about *Growing Pains* had it not been for DiCaprio, although I did find a pleasant surprise in Carol Seaver's character.

Whether gushing over DiCaprio's portrayal of Arthur Rimbaud (another pleasant surprise) in *Total Eclipse* or renting *My Own Private Idaho*, I felt I had to explore queerness in secret through the media and in solitude, never uttering a word to anyone about how much these screen crushes were helping me find solid ground. I'd watch movies and TV in the basement of my childhood home, at the time a more isolated domain than my own bedroom, to learn about queer experiences through queer-identifying characters. It was a lonely way to learn.

Perhaps it was also lonely because the environment where I was growing up was an isolated neighborhood, where all the other children were into straight crushes and into talking about these straight crushes, and there was no other girl or boy—and certainly no adult—to whom I could turn to talk about my queer crushes. This extended beyond my neighborhood, to school, to sports teams, to places where it seemed every boy and girl did their part in showing off how normal they were.

As to whether things might've been easier for me had I made queer friends or had come out when I thought I was supposed to (in adolescence), I can't say, but I can say for certain that feeling as if I were alone in my experience affected the way I treated myself, the way I treated male friendships, and the way I treated relationships as I got older.

I came out at twenty, after moving into my first apartment as a sophomore in college. I called my sisters and told my closest friends in person if I could, calling some others. (Everyone was accepting, or had already suspected.) It was then that I began to queer-identify, on a sunny afternoon in my parents' backyard with a cordless phone pressed to my ear. I'd needed language, needed to be able to *say* the words, and I thought that once I'd found them everything else would fall into place.

When I entered community college I found an openly gay English professor who turned out to be pivotal to my life, and I latched onto him. Every English class I took during my first two years of college was with him, and I latched, in part, because I needed someone who could mentor my queerness.

As if queerness could be mentored, that is. I was under the impression that identities could be learned, that someone could teach me how to be queer like Eminem had learned to be black, and that if I only *listened* I could come into my own with the help of an experienced teacher. I'd found this teacher, I thought, and I spent semester after semester in his classes, learning not only about English but about how to be comfortable in my skin.

My professor and I didn't see each other only in class. I often visited him during his office hours, and he even read the short stories I'd written for fun, giving me critical but kind feedback. He helped me figure out where to finish my degree, and he never seemed to give me only academic advice, but advice somehow tied to life. One thing I'll never forget him telling me, on a day when we discussed college: "Be careful about making plans, because everything changes when you meet someone."

Regardless of the support from those people who loved me when I did choose to come out, having a mentor in my life who queer-identified made me comfortable with myself in ways no one else did or could. I never wrote about my queerness, nor was I open in any of my professor's classes, but knowing I had access to someone who was like me, in some way, preceded the need for openness.

He was also, perhaps, the first queer person I'd ever met in Normal. We spread rumors in junior high about our math teacher being a lesbian, though I don't remember her ever bringing a partner to family events put on by the school, and so any rumors were just that. But this man was *out*: he had a partner with whom he'd been for tens of years; they had a daughter together; and when I was his student I got to hear about him welcoming his first grandchild. I couldn't have known, really, what "gay pride" meant then, but I was sure that I saw it in him.

Little did I know that I'd move to Chicago after a little over a year of being out in Normal. Not only would I choose not to have a second coming-out party in Chicago, but I'd slip back into that compulsory behavior; whether in my new dorm building or in the bar across the street, I'd pass for straight as best as I could, afraid that who I was at home wouldn't fly in a city. I was afraid any harassment might be worse. By staying out to my friends at home but keeping mum with the new ones I'd made in Chicago, I explored my sexuality in embarrassing ways; in ways I'm still shy to admit.

When I got to the city I felt there was too much pressure, if you were queer, to join groups of others like yourself. Too much pressure to join a community. Too much pressure to be visible. I hadn't been out for long enough, was only out to my sisters and to my friends at home, and I wasn't ready to throw myself into student groups on campus or even the city's queer neighborhoods. I was trusting with people who asked, though never forthcoming about my sexuality. I wasn't ready for any kind of queer visibility.

Let's just call it like it is: I went back into the closet. An honest life in Chicago would've meant not having to wait for someone to ask whether or not I was straight. I didn't want to wear my sexuality on my sleeve, but when others said to me, "I'm gay!" or, "I'm bi!" I at least could've said, "I am, too!" and maybe could've made some instant friends. Being out, the way I was at home, would've required more dialogue than I had the courage to engage in.

What I didn't realize until Chicago, what I didn't understand to be an advantage of bisexuality, was that it gave me the ability to pass as straight. I'd already been passing for most of my life, and I didn't see any real harm in suppressing the feelings that would've alienated me from the boys I'd learned to model myself after in order to feel safe. I remember these boys—particularly from junior high—none of whom I ever had crushes on but with whom I hung out playing video games or soccer or watching movies and anime. I thought this was more than just the meaning of boyhood, that it was normative boyhood, and mimicking every straight boy's behavior made me feel a little less like myself and a little more a part of the group. This resurfaced in Chicago, when the young men I befriended became old enough to drink and share details of their drunk and sober sex lives, and when I thought I'd need material for stories. And although I've never picked up a woman in a bar, there were women already in my life whom I wooed for the sake of experience. In retrospect I wish I'd found more love instead.

Being around young straight men in Chicago reminded me of playing team sports back in Normal. I grew up in sport, from Tee Ball to varsity soccer, and I learned that part of being on a team wasn't just about having the ability to throw or kick a ball but also about the ability to talk about girls. As a child and as a teen, however much I already felt I stood out by being the only black player, or nowhere near the best player on the team, I felt offset further by having to wiggle my way into straight-boy talk. When we weren't talking about the game on the sidelines, we talked about girls.

Like being on a sports team full of boys, living in the city was too encouraging of normalcy. It somehow didn't occur to me that there were others who were also new to the city, also queer, and I wanted to find a normalcy not *within* queerness but separate from it, a way to enact the beautiful anonymity that a city provides. I felt I couldn't do so while being out and proud.

When bisexuals pass as straight, especially when in heterosexual relationships, it's easy to claim that it isn't privilege but erasure, an assimilation into a straight position in a heteronormative culture. It lets us presume we can "see" who's queer and who's not by pointing out who's holding whose hand in public, who looks more femme than butch, or who "dresses gay" and who doesn't. These assumptions alienate queers, we say, because the ability to be invisible is a byproduct of heteronormativity rather than a privilege.

When I look at myself, I can't totally buy this. Can't assimilation be simultaneously byproduct and privilege? Like our ability to code-switch in language, is my attraction to both women and men a kind of switching of an identity code, a way of engaging in multiple presentations of myself? Is it really that much different from, say, being able to move back and forth between my family's black jargon and my own central Illinois white English?

When my nephew, still on the cusp of adolescence, once asked me if I was gay, I almost told him, "Sometimes," which would have been untrue. Instead I explained my queerness to him with an analogy I'd stolen from the internet: I told him that bisexual people are like fold-out couches, which are not *sometimes* couches and *sometimes* beds but always both at once. They do not skip between Column A and Column B but instead hold permanent residence in Column C.

I wish I'd had this analogy in my pocket when I was younger. It helped illuminate for me that to be a fold-out couch is advantageous, a way to partly control others' perceptions of myself. In essence, not having to explain my residence in Column C— being able to tuck a part of myself away, in other words—made life easier, in a way that seemed as clean as proclaiming that one is "only" gay or straight.

Maybe to a degree I've also held onto this cleanliness by using a word like "queer" rather than "bisexual" to describe my identity and orientation. But while it's a word that feels just as accurate as "bisexual" would, I don't like "bisexual"—it feels too much to me like a word used in a doctor's office, a clinical term written robotically on a form. (Not to mention that it implies that gender is binary.) I do like "queer" because it works as an umbrella term, giving me a way to respond, "I am, too!" "Queer" isn't riddled with details, and it doesn't invite any further questions.

I wish someone had told me when I was a boy that it was okay for me to like other boys. And girls. And I wish someone had told me I wouldn't have to make up my mind. But inhabiting a conservative environment like my hometown, or even hyper-active environments like my first Chicago neighborhoods, isn't conducive to solving a queer boy's confusion, isn't conducive to making him comfortable, and it doesn't help him move between social codes. Looking back now, it seems like I always inhabited confusing spaces, whether a sports team, a junior high cafeteria, or a dorm across the street from a bar.

If asked why I remained closeted in Chicago for so long, I'd have to give the same answer I would give if asked why it took me twenty years to come out at home: fear and convenience. Although I did figure *myself* out, discerning my environment was a much slower process, and one I felt I needed to internalize rather than express. And it was difficult to figure out how to be confident in an identity that's both queer and a minority in a place where my junior high and high school were on the same street, my community college was around the corner, and there was a whole lot of corn in between.

While this is neither an exaggeration of space nor of topography, I've used it as an excuse for my lack of bravery. Growing up I knew only one other queer boy, who wasn't out until high school and who was much more flamboyant than myself; when he came out he seemed surrounded by comfort and friendship (from girls, I should note), not to mention that it took none of us by surprise. This should've given me a clue that, all along, I too might have been in good hands. I wish I'd had that boy's brav-ery, and I wish I hadn't allowed my schools' or my hometown's scrutinizing atmospheres to be suffocating, not just allowing but encouraging me to engage in whatever projection of straightness I could.

Now I write to allay my suffocation. To say to my dear queer readers that I wish I'd been braver, not just for myself but for them as well. And to my dear straight readers, that I now understand my queer posture as a kind of immunity. It has been a certain advantage not to always have to consider sexuality as also being a social position.

I pretend sometimes not to know what it's like to be straight. This is always a lie, because for years I exercised the privileges of my own orientation. My experience has been muddy but invaluable, and it's experience that has helped me gain insight into negotiating identity. But that identity can, in the first place, be a sign that at least some of us can consider the benefits of not only passing and pretending but of being able to fold inward for comfort.

TO REBEL AGAINST MEN

Over the phone with a childhood friend, I learned that my high school varsity soccer team had gotten back together. For the most part, anyway. They're playing indoor soccer now, at a gym in the middle of nowhere at the edge of my hometown, neighbored by an almost always empty movie theater and open fields that separate the town from its airport. From what my friend told me, some of the guys are still happy-go-lucky, some still pensive and quiet, all of them still confident in their physical prowess.

I remember how good it felt when *I* was eighteen to have six-pack abs, to be able to run a mile in just a little over six minutes, to be able to sprint and jump to my heart's content. I remember how it felt as I circled the field or ran its length. I was too confident in the condition of my body.

I imagine the guys today feel just the same, that they still feel confident. I haven't used my body the way they do in years, though, so it would take months of training to get where they are now, if that's even possible. But I still sat with the news of their reunion and wondered what it would be like to be with them, over a decade later, using the muscles and joints of a thirty-something rather than those of a teenager.

When I imagine all of this I'm hesitant, not at the idea of playing with them but at the idea of being *around* them in the first place. I know that we spread like seeds after graduation, many of us going off to college, some to full-time jobs or to the military, and I know these things have changed us. But it's the return to the pose of the puffed chest that furls my brows, the use of another guy's last name in a cool tone, or a pat on the ass, or side bench talks about women and drinking that make me say *No thanks*. As ready and willing as I'd be to play my heart out for them, I'd expend just as much energy trying not to share in our male bonding experience.

I was four when my little sister was born, and I cried when I learned she wasn't a boy. I remember denying it outright when I heard the news, telling my father and oldest sister that I knew they were joking with me, thrashing and wailing in the hallway of our kitchen. I denied it so much because, with two adolescent older sisters, I wanted someone on my male-child team. I wanted a little brother so badly, so desperately, to feel less alone as a boy in my home.

My father was there with me, but I'll put all on the table and say that for twenty years, until I moved out from under my father's roof, I was terrified of him. He wasn't an abusive parent, but he was combustible. Short-fused. Quick-tempered. I also learned growing up that our ideologies never matched, and that he was combative against my sensitive temperament. I was a softie, and an obvious one.

I didn't want to be tough like the boys at school, even though I enjoyed the roughness of play. As a boy I experimented with, without committing to, participating in Tee Ball, baseball, basketball, soccer, inline hockey, wrestling, football, Taekwondo, BMX racing, and aggressive inline skating. I didn't enjoy school, instead preferring to play with tomboy friends around the neighborhood by riding our bikes or climbing trees or sneaking off into the woods. Aside from all of my video gaming, I was an energetic and active little boy who dirtied his clothes and skinned his knees.

As a boy I thought this had nothing to do with gender. There were two other boys in the neighborhood, but they were younger than I, and it took them a while to get big enough to play with me, so I spent all my time with their older sisters. These girls were themselves athletic, at least for a while, so I saw us as equal and thought nothing of our differences—our fears, our dress, our interests—until we all got older. I thought nothing of what it meant to "be a boy."

The lessons I learned from my father, though, worried me. Although fathers often prepare their sons for manhood, everything my father tried to teach me about being a man instead turned me the other way. I saw my father as the very definition and example of the kind of man he wanted me to grow into, and I wouldn't have it. What it meant to be a man, from what I interpreted from his example, was that a man should be tough, a man should be loud, a man should show his anger as his strength and should never cry, should raise his tone and sharpen his glare, and when he's going to punish you he'll make you feel, because of his mightiness, like the smallest, most vulnerable person on this entire giant and scary Earth. Whether or not it was what he intended for me to see, this *was* how I saw my father. And if becoming my father was what it meant for me to become a man, then I never wanted to grow up.

In the 1996 political thriller *City Hall*, there's a scene in which New York City deputy mayor Kevin Calhoun (portrayed by John Cusack) speaks with Mayor John Pappas (portrayed by Al Pacino) in Pappas's office, or maybe sitting next to him in a car, and he advises the mayor to give a political opponent a little distance.

"Distance," Pappas says, "is shit. Distance. . . . Distance is something you do to your enemies. It's a thing of the nineties, to make friends extinct. Distance is the absence of *menschkeit*!"

"Translate that for me," Calhoun says.

"You don't know what *menschkeit* means?"

"No, I don't."

"*Menschkeit*!" Pappas says. "You know. It's something between men. It's about honor. Character. Untranslatable." He calls *menschkeit* "the space between a handshake."

The idea that there could be "something between men" has always gotten under my skin. And though I never tried giving it a name before *menschkeit*, I have always known that I've been against it. Against an honor among men not to rebel against honor but to rebel against men. This isn't to say that *menschkeit* is more concerned with being a man than with being a good person—but in *City Hall*'s idea, in Pappas's handshake space, I have always found discomfort. I've never given a damn about the "solidarity" of male same-genderedness, which I've recognized as machismo, because it has always made me uncomfortable to recognize that I don't fit within it. I don't fit machismo. I don't fit "broing out," shouting along with other men in bars, bumping chests, and pounding fists. I don't fit, for all intents and purposes, closing the space of a handshake with a proud display of my strength.

This is all front-loaded with a number of complicated things: I didn't want to be like my father; I didn't want to be like the bullying boys at school; and I didn't want to be like the male teammates I grew up around—all of whom symbolized masculinity for me and because of whom I've had difficulty accepting manhood.

I have always wanted to be considered beautiful. I was proud of my voice's range when I sang in school plays and musicals as a child. I blushed at lovers in my twenties who complimented the length of my eyelashes and the shape of my fingernails and the smoothness of my skin. I played certain sports and games not based on how good I was at them but because of how good I thought my body looked when I played them. I have always aimed for beauty of the body, which, in my case, has meant inhabiting a male self that is more elegant than it is tough.

For me beauty has always been about elegance within effort-lessness. It lies in the things and people who aren't reaching for it, which might mean that since I have always been reaching I have never been beautiful. But I've used it as artifice anyway: I've used it as a way, perhaps, of tricking myself into believing that I'm not, in fact, reaching.

As a boy, I was always embarrassed when my adult relatives would tell me what a *handsome man* I'd grow into, both because I thought they were untruthful (though polite) and because I didn't like the weight of the word "handsome." I thought they were untruthful because I found myself ugly—being a short kid with spread-out, buck teeth and unkempt hair—and because I thought *handsome* to be generally attributed to men, and if I were going to grow out of my ugliness, I'd want to become *beautiful* instead.

This might be how I found balance in the physical games and sports I played. Because I was good at sports—never an all-star, though not a complete klutz. I found ways to make myself look beautiful on a court or on a field. I found ways to let my body move spectacularly through space, giving me the middle ground I needed between being a boy and being a beauty. I didn't play for competition like other boys, didn't care when we lost (and was just neutral when we won), and was a selfish team player in that I always wanted to be a part of these teams not for camaraderie but for a physical challenge: for the simple end goal of looking beautiful in play.

There used to be pictures of me as a teenage athlete hanging up in the basement of my parents' former house. Pictures I sometimes wished I could get rid of because I was embarrassed by what I tried to perform in them. There was a picture of me standing with my arms crossed, wearing an emotionless expression. A picture where I'm taking a knee behind my soccer ball. There was one of my senior pictures, in which I'm wearing an athletic warm-up jacket because it happened to be a game day, and I chose to dress in athletic rather than formal attire.

What I saw when looking at those pictures was an artificial self. I always loved being athletic but hated being an *athlete*, hated letting adjective transform into noun, into my identity as a part of what others got to see when they looked at me. The gym shoes, the jeans, the jacket—they were all rhetorical bits of my fashion that I felt misrepresented me to a gazing, teenage audience.

These bits presented me as harder than I was. Sure, my body was hard, and strong and agile and fast, but I still never felt quite as "manly" as my adolescent body did. What did my adolescent body feel? It felt growth in its height and width. It felt horniness. It felt clarity—in the arteries, in the heart, in the lungs—a clarity that contributed to a personal fable of invincibility. But on the inside, I felt soft: sensitive to criticism of my overt politeness, of my intellect, of my wish to express my insides (over the phone, in letters, in late-night internet chats).

My father used to apologize to me for the way he tried to raise me. He used to say that, because he didn't have a father growing up, he had no idea how to be one to a son. But I think there's less to being a *father* here than there is to being a *man*, and I can only begin to guess at how my father learned about the parameters of manhood with my grandfather in absentia.

I worry and wonder about my own lessons in manhood, both about the ones I've learned and the ones I'll teach. I worry because I'm secure in my manhood, which might just mean that I've been cocky. Isn't cockiness, though, all too often the measure of a man? Is my overconfidence in my ability to move between being cute or soft or boyish, and a serious male adult, for example, also my most male quality? I know that I'm afraid to peacock, to show off my own feathers.

These feathers, I'm sure, are far more bold than beautiful.

EVER THE MOTH

My friend Kristen shared a birthday with Siddhartha Gautama. Or she at least shared the birthday observed in many (if not most) Eastern temples, so I wanted to buy her a book on Buddhism. She'd be turning twenty, my age, and our friendship began when we were living in Normal, around discussions of religion since we were both enrolled in religion classes at the same time, not to mention her being a student in a Japanese class I was a TA for as a sophomore in college. I thought she was smart, funny, awkward, and kind—all things I found disarming and perfect reasons for a friendship.

We were walking through a used bookstore on Illinois State's campus one day when I found something I thought looked perfect for her: a collection of writings on Mahayana Buddhism by ancient priests. The book jacket's plastic protector gave it the look and feel of a library edition, and her face was gleaming as I held it up.

She said one thing to me: "If you get that . . . I might have to do something." I paused, arrested. Up for any surprise she might've had in mind.

I bought the book. When we left the store, she hugged me when I handed it to her, then gave me a quick peck on the lips. I blushed.

I drove her back to her dorm in my Jeep. I parked by the front entrance, and we sat for a few minutes, talking as we prepared for an awkward goodbye. Then another surprise: she unlatched her seatbelt, leaned into me, and kissed me again, this time more than a peck. This time, with both of our eyes closed, I kissed her back.

I'll say now that she had a boyfriend, that this is our story in a semester's span: We met in class and became friends. She had had a boyfriend, who died of heart failure. She mourned, and as I supported her we grew closer. She got a new boyfriend. She said she didn't like him. She kissed me.

I justified kissing her back by remembering that we were already close—I felt, to be frank, more important than the new boyfriend she claimed not to like. Near the end of our semester we began an affair, and she gave me my first regular set of intimacies, my first time learning to keep certain kinds of secrets, and the first rush of both. I began to learn what I was capable of behind closed doors.

After we kissed I drove back to my apartment to tell Jeremy, my oldest friend and, at the time, my roommate, because I was panicked about her having a boyfriend. I worried about what I'd done, worried that I'd set myself up for wearing a kind of scarlet letter because we lived in a town where people knew each others business.

I came to find, however, that I'd given my palate a sample of something I would grow a taste for throughout the years following. What I didn't anticipate was that I would enjoy the infidelity with Kristen, and that over the next half decade I would have ten more affairs.[1]

Sick with the flu during the winter of my sophomore year, the same semester I met Kristen, I held a Woody Allen movie marathon in my apartment after having been introduced to Allen through a friend who told me to watch *Annie Hall*. The marathon took a couple of days, and it was one I considered a success. In a way, I've continued the marathon for years, and to this day I've counted on IMDb just four of the films he's written *and* directed that I have yet to see.

What I noticed during the marathon was that in many of Allen's films, people cheat on their partner.

At the same time I was falling in love with Allen's work, Milan Kundera, whose writing also often includes infidelity, became my favorite living author. *The Unbearable Lightness of Being*, *Ignorance*, and *The Book of Laughter and Forgetting* began to shape my views on life and literature. I was a psychology major then, but preparing to change schools and foray into creative writing, and I found myself nudged forward by two artists whose work might best be described as complicated. I learned to love their work because of the way the work handled issues of moral complexity, which were new for me.

While there are lessons we learn from experience, some lessons, about the grayer areas of life, can be passed down through speculative art. For me Allen's and Kundera's art displayed viewpoints about life that stretched from one work to the next, and they were viewpoints that began to influence my own. I'm not saying I began an affair because a few books and movies showed me the way. In fact art likely would have been the last thing to shape my moral outlook then: I was morally rigid when I was younger, wasn't a drinker until twenty-one, shunned anyone smoking pot or cigarettes or having sex in high school, and so on. I knew, or thought I knew, the direction my moral compass pointed, and I hadn't done much dabbling in liminal space. The gray area was new to me, and I was learning to like it.

Fast-forward a few months from Kristen to a friend's twenty-first birthday party. There were three of us: two young women and myself, sitting in a dimly lit bar in downtown Chicago having a little more to drink than we should have (as is often the case with twenty-first birthdays). I flirted a bit, my friend flirted back, and when we were done drinking I promised her friend that I'd get her back to her dorm room, which was on the floor above mine. We got so very close to sex that night, but I didn't have a condom, we were fumbling around, and her roommates were home. It wasn't until we'd sobered up a bit that any of the guilt began to set in for her, as she had a long-distance boyfriend, a fact I'd been aware of going into the night but that I didn't let stop me because I'd done this before. This was my second infidelity.

In later months and years there'd be a woman in a black-painted bathroom stall in a gay club in Prague, a woman with a negligent and clueless boyfriend, a woman with an unstable boyfriend, women I was spontaneous with, women I fell in love with, and here's the et cetera. A roommate of mine made me count once at dinner, asking me flat-out how many people I'd kissed. I began a tally then, and by twenty-six I'd kissed twenty-six people: eleven partnered women, fourteen single women, and one man. I realized then that I was a serial kisser, and that this serial kissing felt better, a bit more artificially righteous than if it had been serial sex, as kissing—and along with it the ability not to go any further—gave me a sense of control, a sense of being able to check in with both myself and others about how much I liked someone. Kissing became easy as pie; kissing was a flagship of mine for years, and it wasn't just kissing but the addition of infidelity that I felt I got good at. That I felt good about.

It was a source of self-confidence.

For twenty years I hadn't liked a single thing about myself. I was histrionic; I talked too much. I was clingy and fake, always performing behind one façade or another. As a boy, I picked the qualities I liked most about the other kids in my classes and tried adopting them, unaware of the fact that they were inimitable. I wanted to be well-liked, and I overcompensated by trying to be funny or by being polite with everyone, thinking it would earn their friendship. (A note to self: Being polite will not necessarily make someone like you.)

I felt I *had* to be polite, had to put people at ease because I saw the world, at least the world the way my parents had presented it to me, as a world that would be wary of me. It would be wary most tangibly of my black maleness, but also of my queerness (i.e., bisexuality), and I thought politeness was the only defense I had against a world that was taught to hate me. Especially when the world, where I lived in Illinois, both looked and was nothing like me.

I used my politeness to gain close friends: I wanted people I could call after school and talk on the phone with for hours (and with some, I did) because I wasn't aware that this wasn't really how teenagers liked to get to know each other. I told many lies as a boy and as a teen, not outright crying wolf but lying through exaggerated detail, for the sake of a better story. In short, I was annoying. Everyone, myself included, knew it.

So when a woman with a boyfriend could look at me and say *I prefer you*, I went with it. I went with it for years, taking the qualities my lovers claimed to like about me and honing them, using them to my advantage in any social situation I could—a measure of gamesmanship, for sure, and a desire to be socially successful. I learned how to like myself by having a love life.

My hamartia, were I an actual hero, would be my need to appear without blemishes. To keep them hidden so that no one could point out the imperfections I saw in myself daily. I continued performing my politeness, not just for the above reasons but also because I don't like being figured out. I've had trouble trusting others with the same knowledge of me that I have of myself.

For example, I lived with two women during my senior year of college. One day, outside of class, I ran into one of them in the hallway and for some reason chatted with her about what she thought was my figurative Achilles heel. She said that I was like "Christmas every day." When I asked her what she meant, she explained that she and my other roommate wondered about my politeness; she said that Christmas was a wonderful thing, but if it occurred every day its meaning would be questioned and its joy would be lost. People would become wary of the intentions behind gift-giving.

My roommates wondering what I was hiding by being polite all the time was a sign that I either needed to stick with my convictions to appease myself or, to appease my roommates, quit being polite so often. But what politeness hid was a fixation with my own imperfections, a fixation with my insecure need to perform. Word had spread to this particular roommate that I was seeing a woman who had a boyfriend, and she responded that she couldn't see me "doing that kind of thing."

The fact that I spent so much of my young life having self-loathing or being self-defeatist made me want to hide that I hadn't liked myself for so long. I thought: How would I make any friends with nothing attractive to advertise? Who would want to be my friend if they knew what I saw in myself? I had to lie. I had to pretend to be happier than I was, had to be able to peacock my merits in order to bring people into my life. And this was all happening at a time when I formed a circle of erotic friends all while trying to maintain the ruse of being upright, never deceptive, never sitting on a moral fence.

In writing about my infidelities here I feel I've advertised a weakness. But I think that's the point. When we write about our lives we have a responsibility to own up to our decisions, to learn to play the fiddle as we watch our own Rome burn. "The writer must be in it," Arthur Miller once said in an interview. "He can't be to one side of it, ever. He has to be endangered by it. His own attitudes have to be tested in it. The best work that anybody ever writes is the work that is on the verge of embarrassing him, always." I wonder what embarrassment adds when we write our nonfiction. Or conversely, perform within our lives, our fictions.

Rossi Street in St. Petersburg, Russia, is known to its locals as "The Street of Ideal Proportions." I've never seen the street in person, have never been to St. Petersburg, and I'll probably never visit. I learned about the street from the film *Les poupees russes* (2005), in which the street, three sides lined by buildings, is described as being 25 meters wide, the buildings 25 meters high and 250 meters long. In the film the street is likened to "the ideal woman."

I've met this street many times in my life. The last time was at a university in Prague where I studied, and where I met a woman from Houston. She was calm, brilliant, articulate, humble. A brunette with pale skin, a good deal smarter than I, and who told B-grade jokes, saying things like, "I've never met a semicolon I didn't like," and who therefore fit the dimensions of Rossi Street for me. In retrospect there were parts of her (her demeanor, her attire) that reminded me of the most confident moments of Diane Keaton's Annie Hall. I wanted nothing more than to know her but thought throughout the beginning of our friendship about the real reasons why.

There are people in the world we get to know so little that they transcend the realm of lovely and enter the realm of perfect. Men and women who seem to fulfill our desires but in reality may snore in their sleep. May snort when they laugh. May smack their gum or keep up with the Kardashians. Knowing a person for such a short time, we allow their image to remain untarnished.

This is a major problem for me, because I get crushes disgustingly, embarrassingly easy. I'm quite the sucker, you see. And as the nature of my love is often unrequited, I've had many more crushes than I've had fruitful loves: Rossi Street crushes, intellectual crushes, work crushes, celebrity crushes (I've had lasting ones on Audrey Hepburn, Mandy Moore, and Emily Mortimer), college crushes, graduate school crushes. One of the easiest things in the world for me is to find some twinkle in another person's humanity and let it carry me adrift. Sometimes these crushes are asexual, sometimes hetero- and sometimes homo-, but they all still give me some starry-eyed gaze.

This is because, I think, I am always the moth and never the flame. I am so uncomfortable being the flame. When people tell me they've fallen for me, my first thoughts are all the reasons they shouldn't. *Their* flame, their fire, shines a light on the things I find wonderful about them as an other (significant or otherwise), as well as the distortions I see in myself.

I think this might be more the result of my self-shame than an issue of my starry-eyedness and whether I've done the things I've done in lust because I've been ashamed of myself for so long. I've looked for validation through the sometimes shallow affections of others, and it's because I've idealized the other, the feminine other in particular, in times when I've found so little to idealize in myself.

Growing up the only boy with three sisters, I always wanted to be one of the girls. I idealized them because they gave me a sense of safety and comfort that I never felt I received from my father, or from any other men, for that matter. Because of my soft temperament as a boy, I felt I fit much better with the girls, their gentle voices and squeaky laughter so much closer to my childhood self.

At times I felt like I was supposed to be ashamed of this idealization. I felt that whenever I was being honest with myself about who I wanted to be or become that I secretly disappointed my adult male relatives, railing against any hardness they might've wished I'd develop while I was growing up. I had no shame, though, in idealizing the feminine, and I knew that any real shame was tied instead to the betrayal of my softness as a boy.

In *A History of Feminist Literary Criticism*, Linda Anderson writes, "Shame is not to do with repression so much as with a desire to communicate: it indicates both a break in the circuit of communication and a 'desire to reconstitute the interpersonal bridge.' Shame could be seen, therefore, as poised at a threshold, looking both ways, toward a painful individualism and towards the pleasure of connection." I found both "painful individualism" and "the pleasure of connection" early on, spending most of my time with my oldest sister, Melissa, while my parents worked and were, I felt, often absent. I give her credit for being my ultimate babysitter, the present one, the pseudo-Freudian model for what I'd look for in my protectors later on.

I remember when Melissa left us. I remember an Amtrak train platform in Chicago, my parents and my baby sister and me in tow, bidding farewell as she prepared to meet her new husband in California. I was about eight, I think. And I remember crying—no, weeping, bawling out of fear of being left alone with my parents and without my big sister, as she had become my anchor and guardian. I remember every ounce of desperation in my tears and voice that day, the way they poured out into an echoey, concrete hall of train platforms that seemed to be stealing my sister.

As I grew through elementary school, junior high, high school, every girl I intentionally befriended was to help fill this childhood vacancy. If boys love their mothers, I defied this by loving Melissa, and I filled my life with characteristic resemblances of her to the point of bursting. My sister, a woman, made me feel safe, and this was all I sought until I felt ready enough to face the world on my own. To face it without needing a girl or a woman to protect me.

Helping a woman be happy came to be something that contained a very sharp sense of having done something right, which wasn't a feeling I had much as a boy. I've loved having relationships, romantic and otherwise, with women, because they're so much easier for me than any kind of relationship with a man. I don't feel dishonest in saying that I haven't trusted men, and encountering any man who isn't at least somewhat effeminate makes me feel as if I'm thrust into competition, which is a feeling I hate because I'm made so viscerally uncomfortable by machismo. I do not feel in competition with women, however, and I do not feel in competition with effeminate men, straight or not.

I've familiarized myself with the concept of establishing an other and with seeking authority and validation from this other. I also know about establishing myself as an other. I wonder at times whether, because I've always felt othered—never tall enough, never quite black enough, never masculine enough, never hetero or queer enough, and in so many cases not smart enough—I've clung to an othered group for camaraderie. I wonder whether this is the way I learned to establish agency growing up, by seeing how the women in my home and in my life had paved their way, thinking I had to do the same. Is this what I learned? Have all my lessons in agency come from women?

It's difficult to write this without feeling like I'm trying to justify what I've done with my sex life, but maybe that's how I need to make sense of my decisions. "A writer always writes out of difference," according to Nancy Mairs, "not just of gender but of every circumstance, and awareness of her idiosyncrasies is likely to strengthen her work if only because it enhances her control of them." I am striving for control. I'm unsure whether it's masculine or feminine control or a kind of androgynous control, but I need to control something here. I need to feel that I've cognized something, that I've made sense of something, and that by looking back I can move forward with just a little bit of understanding. Mairs continues to ask, paraphrasing Virginia Woolf, "Can one *be* 'woman,' *do* 'woman,' but not *think* 'woman'? And if one can't, will one truly expire?" She adds later that one probably will not expire, but I'm interested in asking the same question of myself as a man. As I get older, will it be important to be, do, and think my gender? And if I cannot separate my thinking about all of this from my maleness, will I expire?

I became attracted to a number of Woody Allen's films because, aside from his (dry) brand of humor, at heart I've always been interested in character studies, and throughout my life I've paid more attention to the complicated relationships in stories than I have to complicated plots. This isn't to say that they're independent of each other, but it's the people who make the story for me.

This has been true to my life as well. The relationships that have taken on the most meaning for me are the ones that haven't been easy, the ones with layers and strings, the relationships that have required me to *think* about them on some meta level, which is also why they have failed. So many of them have failed whenever I've tried to make sense of things when instead I could have just appreciated them, absolving my friend or lover of unnecessary stress.

This was where I felt guilty, with Kristen and with any other infidelity. I felt guilty for trying to create layers where there were none to add—for asking, just after she or any other lover had ended a conversation on the phone with her boyfriend as she lay next to me, how it went. For still, after all that was going on within and between us, trying to be so polite about it.

NOTES

1. "Infidelity," traditionally defined, is a "violation of an understood interpersonal agreement." Why I distinguish it here from "affair" or "adultery" or "indiscretion," for example, is that it requires responsibility. While I know that, by this definition, the infidelities are always *theirs* and not *mine*, here I choose to claim them.

CHICAGO

METROPOLIS

When I moved to Chicago at twenty-one, I moved into a dorm in the Printer's Row neighborhood on the south end of downtown, across the street from a string of bars and a little café. Around the corner was a homeless shelter that all dorm residents were warned to be careful around. It isn't there anymore, but during my first year in Chicago I often found myself walking by the shelter on my way to class or to the subway.

Having grown up in central Illinois in a town surrounded by nothing but open corn and soybean fields, what I thought I knew about city life and the homeless I'd learned from movies and TV. I thought the characters denying their homeless neighbors money were either being too cautious or too selfish. I wanted to be neither and tried to find a middle ground between protecting myself and not being annoyed by the homeless people, who often asked me for money. So I decided to stop carrying cash. That way, at least if I *was* being too cautious or too selfish, I wouldn't also be a liar.

In my hometown I'd carry cash all the time because many restaurants and stores there didn't have credit card machines. In contrast, living in the city almost seemed to require one of two things: making sure that I always had cash or making sure that I never had cash. I wouldn't have an actual credit card until years after I moved to Chicago and found myself using ATMs when I entered places that accepted only cash. This let me carry cash only when I really wanted or needed it. I acknowledged the ability to only sometimes carry cash as a class privilege, and one I exploited as an excited undergraduate who'd just moved to a metropolis.

But it also discouraged me from examining the grittiness around the corner—or, at least, to pretend as if living near a homeless shelter had prepared me for the blemishes of my new city.

Enjoying ice cream with a friend one night on the patio of a Baskin-Robbins near our dorm, we were approached by a man who wasn't homeless but who said he needed money. I don't remember much about how he looked, except that he was black and wore many layers. It was warm enough for us to be on the patio, so his layers might've meant those were all the clothes he had. He stood next to our table for a few minutes as he told us his story, and my friend looked uncomfortable as the man kept talking. Neither of us would finish our ice cream any time soon, it seemed, so I agreed to help the man so he could be on his way.

What he told us was that he was in a lot of money trouble and that his wife was very pregnant. From the patio he pointed to his car—the one detail I can remember is that it was a red sedan—and although I couldn't see her clearly at the time, I could make out a woman sitting in the passenger seat; I couldn't tell if she was pregnant, or if she'd been watching us. I asked my friend to excuse me, then stood up from our table to walk with the man to the KFC next door.

As we walked past his car I could see the woman he'd pointed out earlier, who indeed looked pregnant and made intimate eye contact with the man I was walking with, indicating that she knew him. He and I went inside the KFC, and I asked him what he wanted. I offered him a few choices from the value menu, being a college student who didn't have a lot of money to spend, but he went for the largest bucket of chicken available, saying that his wife gets very hungry (and that he hadn't eaten well in a while either). I think there was also a small side of coleslaw with our order, and maybe a few biscuits. I felt I'd been coerced into feeding a family and convinced myself that it was okay to spend the money because it was for someone else. When the order was ready, I handed it all to the man, who thanked me and walked out of the restaurant and to his car, then drove away as I went back to sit with my friend.

Although nothing violent took place, my actions felt dictated by the man, which was then exacerbated by my friend's physical discomfort. I'd acted, I thought, to protect her from this uneasiness—caused, perhaps, by his poverty, by his maleness, by his blackness. The man might've assumed I was a student because of my youth, khakis, and Polo shirt—these latter two serving as superficial class markers. Because he and I were both black men, and because my friend was a white woman, I thought it might put her at ease to know that I was placing myself between them.

Though the man did not mug us, didn't claim to have a weapon in his pocket, and was somewhat polite throughout the whole ordeal, the desperation in his approach left me feeling I wasn't free to deny him. Perhaps he would've gotten angry, or perhaps my own guilt would've eaten at me, knowing that I could've helped the man but didn't. I had no cash or change on me that I could've given him at the time, so my debit card saved the man and me both, and maybe it saved more than just the two of us: his wife, his baby, my friend. I'm not certain, though, that what I did was an act of kindness, so much as an act of being held hostage by my fear.

As new undergraduates, we were given instructions on how to be safe in the city, which included advice about where not to go and how to walk and when. I remember a few of the rules: Don't talk to strangers on the way to class. Don't wear headphones at night. Don't take public transit too far south of campus, into Chicago's "crime-riddled" South Side. And, just as important, never pull out your wallet in front of someone asking for money. The rationale was that the person could snatch it and run, and then you'd lose more than just the few dollars you'd planned to give away.

There were other rules, I'm sure, but I realize now that the advice our RAS in the dorm gave us was different from the advice I gave when I began teaching in Chicago many years later to my own students, many of whom lived downtown. The RAS' advice didn't make total sense in retrospect—while the headphone rule is a good one, were I to tell my students about the homeless or about the danger zones of the Chicago Transit Authority (CTA), would I be able to do so without feeling as if I'd perpetuated fear through some game of telephone?

Even more than this, I'd come to realize that I was being banned, in essence, from visiting my father's family on the South Side. Although my grandmother had died three years before I began college in the city, I still had aunts, uncles, and cousins who lived in the very part of the city I was being told never to venture toward. I'd complacently let this keep me from visiting, and nine times out of ten I would wait for my parents to come to the city before going anywhere near my extended family's neighborhoods.

When I asked my students to relay what they'd been told about safety in the city, they repeated some of the same things I was told when I first moved there, and I started to wonder where the cycle began and ended. After eight years in Chicago some of that advice now seems like rubbish to me. I can see that my students were told they'd be safest in the city by remaining on campus, or even heading anywhere north of their dorms. They were told, implicitly, that they were safest in Chicago's whitest and most affluent neighborhoods, in the places they might be less often badgered by the city's homeless, its violent, its drug-abused.

Don't go too far south or west. Never ride the train late at night. Is Oak Park even safe? These, among other tips, were what students repeated to me when I asked about the advice they'd received. What seemed strange was that these were students who'd made the choice to attend college at a school in downtown Chicago but were then told that, just like on other campuses, there are ways of avoiding certain dangers. But even other campuses—whether Chicago's Loyola, or DePaul, or UIC—aren't the arboreous bubbles of safety promoted in brochures, and they aren't like the small college towns where everything off campus is expected to be safe and boring.

When I lived in my dorm I was terrified of the rest of the city. It took me forever to feel safe walking home from my night classes when I heard the constant and cacophonous whizzing-by of cars and ambulances. I didn't bother to learn about Chicago's other neighborhoods because I learned to feel safe sticking around my dorm, building a haven out of a single Chicago block. It took me a while to use the city as cities are intended to be used, as vast stretches of possibility and play, and during my first year in Chicago I listened perhaps too much to all those who gave me warnings. I was there for school alone, I'd decided, and the rest of the city was made for those who were willing to sever their roots, whatever those may have been.

"But what good are roots if you can't take them with you?" Gertrude Stein once said, when asked if she was afraid of losing her sense of being American after living in France for so many years. While living in Chicago never put me in any danger of losing my Americanness, I did take with me what I felt were my own roots via the mentality of being from a rural college town. I took corn with me, and central Illinois politeness, and the perception of many things as being either black or white, thinking that as long as I clung to my hometown I could remain the same person I'd always been.

Whenever I assigned my students Joan Didion's "Goodbye to All That," as a class we found ourselves comparing Didion's move to New York with our own moves to Chicago. This isn't to say that the two cities are comparable, but Didion's move to New York at twenty and mine to Chicago at twenty-one are always juggled side-by-side in my head, as I look upon my first year in the city and regard my own naïveté. "Was anyone ever so young?" Didion asks in her essay, and I feel at times that I could not have been younger.

I find camaraderie with a writer like Didion because we both lived in our cities for eight years (though she intended to stay for just six months, and I intended to stay for two years). I suppose I could just ask them, but I still wonder how many of my other friends, from college or from graduate school, convinced themselves they'd just be passing through the city but found that they'd become more than transients. Do all cities have such a vacuuming quality? Do they inhale the naïve, just to hold them for ransom?

I can remember visiting my friend Lisa one night in her dorm room; we chatted for a bit about my second-guessing my move to the city. I went to Lisa because she was a Chicago native and because I felt she was the one person with whom I could talk about my newfound metropolitan anxieties. I told her about my nighttime fears, about my aversion to asphalt and noise and skyscrapers, and I told her that, had I not found myself in such an academically favorable position, I would've left. I'd convinced her, and myself, that I could stay only for as long as college lasted. Yet I hung around for much, much longer.

In the few months before moving to Chicago, my oldest friend, Jeremy, and I would sometimes take weekend trips to the city to help me preview it, and we always stayed with a friend of ours who was attending the college I was planning to transfer to. On these trips we were awed by the possibility of a nightlife—the beauty of streetlights was never so obvious as when we visited Chicago, and it was just one thing among many that made me excited to move.

During one visit we met a homeless man at an intersection near Millennium Park. I remember our meeting being one that shocked me into a reality far different from the one portrayed on TV and in movies. I wish I could remember everything about that man, but I can recall only a few details. He was tall and big, with a large beard, and made me imagine a black Hagrid (of *Harry Potter* fame), and his clothes looked more worn than dirty. I believe he talked about music—that he used to be a musician—and though he told us how he ended up on the streets, I no longer remember why. But I do remember feeling that he hadn't done anything "bad."

I also remember that Jeremy was the one who engaged him in conversation, not me, and I wanted secretly, perhaps telepathically, to tell him to be careful, not to give away any information or money, and for us to cross the street as soon as the light turned. But the man was gentle and harmless, and I ended up imagining his situation being easier somewhere else—not that homelessness is easy anywhere, but I thought that had I given him a one-way ticket to, say, my hometown, he might've fared better there than in the city. He could have found help from organizations like the YMCA, from local food banks, from places that could hide him from the wind and the cold. His fortunes might have improved, given that, in a place much smaller than Chicago, there'd be fewer people who could simply pass him by.

It took a while for me to figure out what and whom to listen to when told what to be afraid of in the city. It's peculiar that this city is one that came with so many warnings. Chicago wasn't a city that sold itself. It didn't tell its new residents (or at least it didn't tell *me*) about beauty or culture or about how the city was a gastro paradise. It didn't tell me about the diversity of its neighborhoods or the scenic walks the city invites. These were all things I had to learn firsthand, by getting lost or by taking impromptu trips on the CTA to random neighborhoods or attending events that required I leave whatever little bubble I'd built.

Had I chosen a college in New York, I wonder whether it would have warned me just as much. What about Los Angeles or Houston? Or Philadelphia? I've heard it said that to be proud of showing off social bruises is an American thing, that it's unique to us to want to talk about how bad we've got it, and Chicago showed off more bruises than it seemed to conceal. Was Chicago therefore a more American city because it touted its gritty realities? Or, I wonder, was there something else there, perhaps more ominous, that I should've seen when I looked at the city's façade?

GREEN AND GRAY

Chicago has become very green to me. What I mean is that I've chosen, for years, to live only in its greener neighborhoods. I've done this for many reasons. One is that they remind me of my hometown, a place with abundant trees, corn, and soybeans—where green was the town's most prominent color, followed by yellow. Another reason is that green neighborhoods feel, somehow, safer than gray ones. More pacifying. I'd rather live in a green neighborhood than in a neighborhood covered by asphalt because it's relaxing to see the natural things that were once available to me in my twenty-one years before moving to the city. It feels right that I reside in a neighborhood filled with trees and grass because I can't stand ubiquitous concrete.

I also used to think that choosing green neighborhoods was the result of growing up in a predominantly white town and that green neighborhoods meant more affluence, and this was something I wanted to pretend to be a part of. I wanted to pretend that I could afford to live in these neighborhoods with ease, wanted to pretend that I was just like the other people who lived in these neighborhoods, and that I had overcome Chicago's blatant fiscal segregation. I know that it's tricky, especially in Chicago, to talk about class without also talking about race; even though I'm black, it isn't my focus here. I'll try anyway, because I need to figure out how I've navigated class in the first city where I was actually independent.

I live in an apartment across the street from a park called Palmer Square. There's a dirt trail here that goes around the entire square that, every day, I see people walk and jog on. I know this trail makes a one-mile journey when circled twice. Mothers bring their strollers here, walking with their infants and toddlers as they exercise in expensive-looking, skintight attire: stretchy pants and sports bras in the summer, stretchy pants and fleece in the winter. There's a smaller park in the middle of this one where the ground is different from the dirt and the grass around the rest of the square; it isn't a park you'd see with a playground, a swing set and a merry-go-round and a slide or two. It's engineered to be softer, pliable, so that the children who fall will hurt themselves less easily. When I stand on it, the weight of my body leaves a temporary imprint that cements the fact that I shouldn't be there, that I'm really too big to be there. That I'm trespassing on a child's territory, happy to be bouncy when I know I should be somewhere else.

I live here because I can look out the window of my living room and see the park and the people playing Frisbee and walking and jogging in their skintight clothing. I live here because all the green, the trees and the grass and even the weeds, makes me feel more at home than other Chicago neighborhoods I've lived in, with shiny lights and bustling taxis, and because there's more peace and quiet here than in those neighborhoods. I live here because I can afford to and because I've been at a place in my life lately where I'm exploiting everything I can afford.

In college I once lived in a studio apartment in Lincoln Park that cost $575 a month. It wasn't a closet by any means, but the fact that the kitchen and the living space weren't separated by anything made it feel a little cramped. At least, I would tell myself, the bathroom isn't always in view; at least it's blocked off by some semblance of a hallway.

I lived there mostly because I wanted to establish myself in a place that felt palpably different and independent from anywhere else I'd lived. Before I moved into the studio I had been in Prague, and when I returned I began looking for places to live alone in Chicago; Lincoln Park was where I settled. I lived on a tree-lined street, where people jogged and pushed their strollers, and I felt like I'd settled into city life without feeling like I was *in* the city. I felt better, basically, by living around yuppies.

These were people who, just a few years my senior, were fine-dining and drinking to their hearts' content. People who could afford to. I was twenty-two when I moved into this neighborhood, and affluence wasn't an apparent issue with any neighbors my age or who were just a bit older. I did wonder, though, how many of them might have been faking it, the way I was—who might have been in debt the way I was but were still showing off a comfy façade. I had a part-time job and student loan money to live on while I feigned the comfort of my living situation. I couldn't actually afford a $575/month apartment, nor could I afford to buy groceries anywhere in the neighborhood except for a somewhat basic market around the corner.

I credit my decision-making here to something I hate thinking and talking about: my relationship to money. And I credit my contempt for this relationship to my constantly thinking about it. It isn't that I grew up poor and was therefore always forced to think about money; in fact I grew up in a very comfy middle-class household, with video game consoles and a TV in almost every room and more than enough food in the fridge. But my parents did grow up poor. My parents are the bootstrap type, who grew up with multiple siblings under the same roof helping to care for their immediate families, while my grandparents brought in what little money they made. And they remained poor until their mid-thirties, eventually becoming concrete examples of upward mobility.

My oldest sister once wrote on Facebook, "I am thankful for a mother and father who taught me how to cook. Even when I was a child and we were so poor that we picked dandelion greens from the field near our apartment, ate government cheese, puffed rice, and those huge mini wheats in a box; when my mother made beans and rice and used the leftover rice in the morning with butter, sugar, and milk to make breakfast, I have never truly gone hungry. Now I am thankful that I can take 5 dollars, if that's all I have left, and feed my family well."

This is a portrait of my parents that I have never seen and will probably never see. Their story is that they were born and raised poor. Even when they went away to college, met, married, and started a family, they struggled. My older sisters are nine and fourteen years older than I, and I'm told the gap between us exists because my parents were waiting until they could afford me; they were waiting until they could perceive some kind of comfort within the new family they'd raised. In short, I exist because of money.

I once tried to find the house where I grew up, searching on a friend's iPad. The satellite view worked, for the most part, but Google's van still hadn't driven through my childhood streets. The picture on the screen (the satellite view) shows three streets, mine the connecting bridge of a μ (but which, growing up, I always thought was an H), and my childhood home sits just slightly off-center in this bridge. I'm amused by the fact that for most of my life I'd pictured my house and neighborhood one way, but with Google's existence everything has changed.

Surrounding this μ is a grove, which from the ground I know to be the woods that I was always told were dangerous. Was told not to enter at any time. But these woods were so green, so inviting, that there was no way my friends and I could keep out. Whether on foot then or on Google now, this is the most prominent thing I know about the neighborhood.

There's a place in Normal my friends and I used to visit that we called the Top of the World. It was the tallest building in town, the top floor of a dormitory, and in college it was where we went to do homework, to make out, to make fun of people's parking and driving, and to ponder a vastness to our home that couldn't be seen from anywhere else. During the right seasons, everything was green from up there. Even when I could spot my parents' neighborhood, which sat across the street from a large patch of yellow corn, from 298 feet above ground the trees blocked the view of any other farms or fields. If there was a view of any field it was green and not yellow, clouding our knowledge of whether it was soy or shrubbery.

It was different from Chicago, where I live now. In Chicago I have friends living in high-rises far taller than the old dorm I'd visit in Normal, and from their balconies all I can see is gray: gray streets, gray sidewalks, gray buildings made of opaque stone. What good is being in a high-rise, I often wonder, when there's nothing below that stirs my heart? Being in a high-rise does this: it dares. It makes me say *C'mon, Mike. I dare you. I dare you to lean. I dare you to know what it's like not to be grounded from* this *high up. I dare you to test your luck.* I'm caught off-balance, made a little uncomfortable by the whispers in my head.

Once, on a bridge, I did dare myself. During a dismal time of my so-called quarter-life crisis I took a drunken two-hour walk home one night in the middle of March from a Lincoln Park bar, which required me to cross a river to get back to my own neighborhood. I stopped on that bridge and stared out at the ice below. I leaned, far. Had I fallen, my body might've broken through the ice, which would then seal itself shut and I'd be pounding at its insides to try and burst through and, after I'd lost all my energy and air, I would've drifted away and my body might not have been found for days. The second I realized I wanted this I cried. I knelt, and I wept. I didn't have any direction in my life, didn't have any money in my life, and foresaw no immediate hope or salvation to take me out of the trough I'd built for myself.

This was in part because, just after college, I had trouble finding work for a while. When I did find work it was as a documentary researcher, for a man who gave me $160 a week in cash, which I used to pay rent, while I put everything else on credit. I lived this way for about seven months, being independent and stubborn and without asking for help, feeling lost and unused, professionally unwanted. Desperate but optimistic enough to be that great fool who'd tell myself, "It won't be like this forever."

My favorite way to spend money is on other people. I love to cover drinks, to cover dinner; I love to buy books and send them off to friends in faraway places (or, just as commonly, buy them for a romantic interest). Money often slips through my fingers when I'm being social, and though it hasn't put me in any trouble yet, I understand my irresponsibility.

I learned at a young age how fun it was to spend money on others, when my father would take me Christmas shopping every year to buy presents for the family. We'd go to the dollar store sometimes, and I could pick out gifts that cost five dollars or less (what were five-dollar items doing at a dollar store anyway?) for my family members—perhaps a cookbook for my mother, a toy for my little sister, a new apron or a set of spoons or picture frames for my older sisters. A cheap battery charger for my father, perhaps. All gifts I thought appropriate for their ages and genders, swept into my own little shopping cart and paid for with money earned by washing cabinets, trimming hedges, and mowing an extra yard.

Though my sisters and I worked for much of our money growing up, we did have an allowance, and like our bedtimes they advanced with age. I remember the importance of my allowance jumping from ten dollars a week to twenty dollars a week because it meant that I was older and more trusted with my own money. Twenty dollars was, to my mind, the perfect sum of money—I could buy a book or a movie or, at times, more than just one action figure. There was so much on the shelves I could buy for twenty dollars, and at around the age of ten or eleven I started to become aware of this. Even now I never feel guilty about purchases under twenty dollars.

Soon after my allowance jumped I was permitted to go out on my own. I began to use the town bus, at the time only twenty-five cents a ride and an easy trip to either of the two malls in town. I could go buy my own blue jeans, my own CDs, or walk into a shop for a big, soft, warm, buttered and salted pretzel with cheese dipping sauce and a pop. It was also time for me to start buying the things that would make me look cool, to look like someone old enough not to be dressed by his parents.

I remember a boy named Tyler, whom I met in seventh grade and who wore the first pair of wide-leg jeans I'd seen in my life. The brand was called JNCO, a flawless product of the late nineties, and I copied him by finding at Wal-Mart a pair of knock-offs I could afford. It wasn't for the style, though; I'd formed an interest at the time in aggressive inline skating, which meant I needed jeans wide enough at their bottoms to fit around my Rollerblades. Though their hems often covered my shoes when I wore them, the point was that they'd meet my skate at the curve of the boot, helping me obey the decorum of never showing off my brand at the skate park. Thus my style in seventh grade: JNCO knock-offs, Airwalk shoes, plain white T-shirt. I felt cool at the skate park because I had no obvious brand loyalty—I thought I was too cool to flaunt, though perhaps a bit shy about my or my parents' purchasing power toward the important brands of my teen subculture.

As a child I thought that because we had the biggest house we were probably the wealthiest (or second-wealthiest) family in our neighborhood. One family down the street from us, the Trowers, had their own business, a tire and auto service shop, and they had more cars in their driveway than we did, which made me think they might've had more money than we did. But the size of our house was the first indication to me that there were many who were worse off than we were, and I knew this because I'd been through those neighborhoods. I'd seen apartments with bars on their windows, houses smaller than ours with less impressive cars in the driveway. Especially in Chicago, where my father's family lived, I perceived the quality of Chicagoans' homes to be lower than ours, less bedazzled than ours. I tried to judge the wealth of others based on the home in which I was growing up, because I wanted to know where I fit in with everyone else in the context of money. I wanted to know where I fit in because I wanted to know that my family was safe, that we would never have to worry or struggle.

My assumptions about my class status as a child in my town were that my family was well-off, but there were many families much worse off, and many others who were much better off. I thought the children at school with holes in their jeans probably came from poorer families than mine. I thought the children who had to bring their own bag lunches probably couldn't afford a cafeteria lunch, at least without some assistance program. Some moms and dads drove cars that weren't as nice as my parents', and some families lived in houses that, clear as day, were falling apart. If you belonged to a family you were supposed to live in a house, not in an apartment or a trailer or anything but a house. And if you were an adult and you rode the bus, it meant you were too poor to own a car.

At the other end of things, there were those with more money than I was able to imagine. As a child I couldn't comprehend the intangible weight of a million dollars and, in a way, still can't as an adult, but I knew there were million-dollar homes in Normal. When my father would take me to the dentist, for example, he'd drive me through a neighborhood called Country Club, a long and winding drive with a golf course on our left and houses the size of small mansions on our right, some with Victorian-style columns or cobblestone driveways in the front, and only one house in the whole neighborhood with just one story. It was because, my father told me, the house's basement had a swimming pool. I didn't doubt his knowledge, but I was in awe anyway at the thought that someone had a pool in their basement, something accessible to those who had (enough) money.

I'm still cementing the judgments I make about money. Thinking about money as an adult is almost depressing, understanding it as something inseparable and symbiotic. It latches on, and we latch on, and, even when we can manage not to think about it for a day, it resurfaces in an attempt to remind us we can't be rid of it. But what if it didn't resurface? What if, in the most absent-minded minutes of our day, we could manage to look at it as something faraway, like we did as children? What does money become when it keeps its distance?

In graduate school I fell in love with Natalia Ginzburg's idealism when I read her book *The Little Virtues*. It was the first time I encountered, either directly or peripherally, someone with whom I shared a perspective on money. In her title essay she writes, "We forget that money, and a liking for saving it, were much less horrible and disgusting things when we were children than they are today; because the more time passes the more disgusting money becomes." She says that the moneybox, the piggy bank, is our first mistake.

The moneybox is a mistake, Ginzburg says, because it accustoms children to a feeling of loneliness when they are without money. It makes them believe money should be hoarded and not spent, when money's function is as a tool for exchange. And it makes them believe that the proper way to think of money is in terms of oneself, wrongly equating two kinds of self-worth.

"As soon as our children begin to go to school we promise them money as a reward if they do well in their lessons," she writes. "This is a mistake. In this way we mix money—which is an ignoble thing—with learning and the pleasures of knowledge, which are admirable and worthy things." I imagine I will not reward my own children with money. With books and films and trips, perhaps, but not with money. I was not rewarded with money for good grades. In fact I did not get good grades, which is probably why money wasn't used as an incentive. But perhaps my parents knew money to be an ignoble thing then—perhaps after living for so long without it, once I was born they knew that had they given me the wrong lessons I would have come to love it and would hold it in a too positive regard were it an automatic reward for my doing well in school. Perhaps my parents educated me very well on the subject of money.

I do not regard money; I treat it as a fake thing thrown about in restaurants and in bars and in bookstores. But I know that it is very real. I know that it's a reason for our wars. I know that Greece and the United States do not play with Monopoly bills. I know that it's the reason the city in which I live, the city I love, is the most segregated metropolis in the country.

I still haven't *really* measured my distance from this money thing. While I regard it as fake but understand it as real, I still haven't established its sentimental connection to my sense of self, which I assume at this point is moot. I'm not worth much money, have never been worth much money, and in fact was probably worth more under my parents' roof living as a dependent, as I could've counted myself as middle-class rather than as some pretender who's scraping by. And I do pretend. I've spent my adult life trying to stay in the class I was born into, but I know it will be a while, if ever, before I can return to my parents' tax bracket.

Growing up, I had fields. Corn and soy. And learning about those fields taught me plenty about how people survive without living in high-rises or in large houses with columns. Third grade geography coupled with an introduction to economics.

I hope that my children's generation, unlike my own, is one that doesn't feel forced to pretend. The farmers in my hometown didn't have to squeeze themselves into another class the way so many of us do with credit and debt, and my hope is that we'll at least have the feigning solved by the time my own children are adults. I'm unsure how comfortable I'll be with a space where the rich are definitely rich but are still pretending to be richer, and the poor do the same with their poverty by pretending to be less poor.

I want my own children to grow up around green, not just to know that it exists. Maybe this is because I've had a depressing relationship with asphalt, with places covered by it and with looming buildings rife with riches. As a child I had many parks nearby, and though there are certainly parks in cities and the children growing up in these cities become very fond of these parks, I want my children's home to be abundant with green. I want to spend my life in green neighborhoods, but I know that, at least in the United States, this often requires money, and will often require more money than I'll have. What I'll hold onto until then, as I attempt to reach my parents' status in my thirties, my forties, and older, is the hope that I can at least be rid of all the metaphorical garb that makes me feel so much, too much, like a great pretender.

GERALDYNE'S ROOM

Geraldyne, my paternal grandmother, died when I was eighteen years old. Lately I've been thinking about her house. I've been trying to remember the way it looked the last time I saw it, because I've noticed the ways some of my own apartments in Chicago over the years have resembled it. What I remember most about her house is that it was always cluttered. It wasn't particularly dirty, but there were always things lying around, from clothes and magazines, to dog toys. The place always felt like a chore to walk through.

This house is on the market for $45,000, with an estimated mortgage of $155 a month. The realtor's description: "Brick Two flat totally rehabbed. One-3 bedroom apartment and One-2 bedroom apartment. New windows, new roof. Two new gas furnaces, Separate electrical meters. New carpets, freshly painted throughout, new kitchen cabinets. Enclosed back porch. Just move in. Laundry hookups for each unit. Unfinished basement."

The house has been for sale, the website says, for four hundred days.

The house, really the apartment on the first floor, was never in what I'd call "bad shape," except for the bathroom, which had rust everywhere. The apartment had an open and unconstricted living room in its front, three bedrooms off to the right when walking through from the front to the back, and a kitchen that resembled plenty of my own: oak cabinets, faux-wood countertops, a two-basin sink.

What I want to say is that the apartment wasn't impressive. Even as a child I always wondered why she lived there. I wondered how my older sisters, who had moved out and had been on their own since I was about ten, could have nicer-looking apartments than Geraldyne, who I thought was supposed to live in a nicer place because she was older. That was how things worked, I thought: people grew up, got good at their jobs, and made enough money to make nice homes for themselves, like my parents had done. How on Earth could my parents have a class marker of a house—always two stories with big yards and, in one case, even a pool—that surpassed my grandmother's? Shouldn't she, as the elder, have been at the top of the ladder? Shouldn't she have been the most visibly established? Shouldn't her home have been more like ours?

I know that Geraldyne worked for a university in Chicago, but I've never known her job title. And her house, in Chicago's West Pullman neighborhood on the far south side near the corner of 118th and Peoria Street, was in a neighborhood that I was told to fear. Was always told was unsafe. It was a predominantly black neighborhood, unlike the neighborhood I'd been spending my childhood in, where mine was the one black family around. Geraldyne's neighborhood, I'd been convinced, was full of bad people, "gangbangers" and "hoodlums" inhabiting it. It was almost a rite of passage for me, when I was allowed to take the garbage out to the alley behind her house by myself, or grab something from our minivan, parked safely out front. I was taught to always be prepared for a mugging, ready to catch someone trying to break into our minivan, ready to be shot at or stabbed on the way to retrieve my Gameboy.

I never wanted to visit Chicago when I was little because I conflated the image of the whole city with my grandmother's block, and I thought that, as in movies and on TV, Chicago was an all-around unsafe place to be in. But the space of Geraldyne's house *was* safe, if only because we were indoors, and this being our only safety was a definite turn-off for me as a child. I could never, for the life of me, figure out why anyone would want to live this way. Why couldn't she have just picked up and moved? Why couldn't she have joined my family in our rural (though collegiate), uncrowded, sprawled-out hometown? Or, if she had stayed in Chicago, why couldn't she have gotten a nicer house on a different block, where people didn't try to kill one another?

I began to understand that Geraldyne was poorer than us, and I confused her lack of actual mobility with what I perceived as her lack of willingness to change. I racked my brain as a child and as a teenager over the reasons why she stayed put, because it seemed to be very much her own choice. If my parents, who had always talked about growing up poor, could improve their status, then why couldn't she?

This raises the question of whether or not my parents were able or willing to help out, a fact of which I'm ignorant. I never asked them. I didn't care. By the time I was eight or nine I was already judging Geraldyne for what I thought was *her* decision to consider the real conditions of her position.

The last time I saw Geraldyne alive I got to miss some school because she was very sick. We made the drive from Normal to Chicago—and this time, at eighteen, I felt competent when I stepped out of the van and onto her sidewalk. I had convinced myself that I was ready, able, and adult enough to deal with *any* trouble because I was preoccupied with the fact of her imminent death, which was heavier than anything else I could've been afraid of.

I walked into the apartment, and as usual I stepped over toys and magazines and clothes as I made my way to hug my relatives. I made my way to Geraldyne's room, the first on the right, and I saw her sitting at the edge of her bed, one dim lamp on the bedside table, my grandmother looking too much like a shadow of herself: heavy breaths, ruffled hair, sagging skin where there was once muscle and fat, a scratchy voice. I answered when she asked me about my life, when she asked me about soccer, about my grades, about what I wanted to do in college. While I know the rest of the family was thinking about her final hours and days, readying themselves for her last moments, I was thinking *This is what you're going to die in.* I was thinking about her dying in filth and clutter, and I felt ashamed by this.

I felt ashamed because I was imagining that her house, and therefore her ending, *could've been so different.* I wanted something more regal for her, a setting that felt just right for a gentle passing. But I felt her house was crap and it upset me that she had lived in it, had tolerated it for so long. I was wishing I'd found her in a place more picturesque. More appropriate for the death of a grandmother.

My maternal grandmother, Betty, has lived in the same house in Waukegan, Illinois, since I was a boy. My mother never lived there; her parents, Betty and Billy, moved into the house when she was about nineteen. Though I haven't visited the house in a while I can say that there's a sizable backyard, a crabapple tree too small and skinny to climb but big enough to notice, and a blue metal swing set with a small slide, and that is how I want it to exist in my memory. In spring and summer when we got bored with the TV my cousins and I would go out to the backyard to swing, challenging one another to go higher and higher. As we got older and bigger our swinging made the metal move, made it creak and wiggle as we pumped back and forth. The challenge eventually stopped being about our trying to see who could swing higher, and more about how long the swing set could actually hold the weight of our growing bodies.

I loved visiting Betty's house as a child, loved to eat the food she'd cook and play with cousins who would later become friends. The house, small for two stories, felt cottage-like, and it sat on a quiet, quaint, tree-lined street. Her neighborhood embodied peacefulness, embodied the American Dream; everyone living on the block had seemingly made it to a middle-class safety: a car in every driveway, a quiet street with sociable neighbors, children playing in their front yards.

I loved visiting this house because it felt the way I thought a grandparent's house was supposed to feel: cozy, safe, warm, floral, idyllic, green, compact, historic, *homey*. Aside from when my grandfather would threaten to pull a switch from the crabapple tree to spank me, I never felt unsafe there. I never feared this place. It was, for all intents and purposes, a refuge where my immediate and extended families came together. It felt like a place where I could be a boy rather than a place where I had to be on my guard.

Out of immaturity we blame others for circumstances we don't like, for circumstances we want to change. I know that the way I felt about Geraldyne was my own immature judgment—but it was also a classist judgment, based on what I now think was an early defined standard of living. And although as a child I perhaps didn't notice markers of class for what they were, a child still notices difference. I judged because Geraldyne's Chicago house was just that: different.

Perhaps this is unfair, and maybe even untrue. I understood that Geraldyne was poor, and thinking about her poverty always used to surface from the fact that she didn't have a (clean) house like my parents, didn't live in a neighborhood like my parents, didn't drive a car like my parents, and never served the food I was used to eating with my parents. I was beginning to understand what I'd seen from the home lives of the other kids I went to school with; it seemed easy to pick out the kids whose parents were well-off from the ones who weren't based on what they wore to school or what their parents drove and how nice their houses looked from the outside. It's safe to say that aside from gender, class prefaced any other social divider I learned about.

I've written about her here as if there was no warmth within my relationship with my father's mother. I don't remember any.

I'm sure that many times I sat on her lap and played with her hair, felt her breath, poked at her face, and listened to her stories, but they're nowhere in my memory. All I can and do remember is how cold and alien her house felt. All I can remember is the danger around it and the fact that her house wasn't in my hometown and that, because of this, I couldn't act the same. Whenever we were in Chicago my father gave me instructions on being attentive and careful in a way he never did at home, and it only incited a fear masked as confident awareness.

Walking down Geraldyne's street I felt more fictitiously adult than anywhere else I'd been in my life because I was acting on edge—acting like a detective of sorts, deconstructing every detail of my surroundings in order to assess the level of safety. I don't want to call it *toughness*, but there was something I performed there in order to feel more ready for the world. When I was a child, acting like an adult meant having this readiness in my pocket.

At home, when my neighbor friends and I used to play house I was always the father because I was the oldest boy in the neighborhood. And my being the father made me act so serious—not in an angry sort of way but in a stern sort of way, making sure the children were homeschooled (we were always homeschooling our children) or that they ate their vegetables when given dinner. Once, while pretending to leave for work one day, I gave my wife a kiss. It was a real kiss, one that left both of us wide-eyed, and after it happened I walked up the stairs to exit my neighbors' basement in order to "go to work," and to walk away from that awkward kiss.

I could never play games like these in Geraldyne's house. Being in Geraldyne's house meant being crowded in with relatives I never felt close to—except for, perhaps ironically, Canadian relatives who would sometimes come down to visit—and feeling either isolated from relatives my age or embarrassed by adults talking about how proud they'd be of my future self. Geraldyne and the rest of the family loved to talk about how much like my father I was and how I would grow up to be just like him, which to me was an obvious delusion at the time because in fact I'd felt that I wouldn't grow up to be anything impressive, and anything I *would* grow up to be would *not* be my father. My identity was displaced in that house, tossed far away from any persona I saw coming.

I remarked to a friend once that it seems everyone around me is not just coupled but also building themselves homes, and this makes me wonder, as I've grown, about which other ways I've been immature in my judgment of a "proper" home life. There *is* this home-building thing I've thought about, because it's been a while since I've lived in a place that felt like a home to me. I'm mostly transplanted or transient somewhere, rarely decorating enough and usually too single to have my apartment shapeshift into the product of a coupling.

I'm thinking here about a woman in Chicago I used to like, who seemed to have built a perfect home for a single person. Her apartment building sat behind another one, and to get to her door I had to walk through a gate and down a narrow sidewalk next to this building—not quite as inviting as a welcome mat or a wreath on the door, but after I'd enter her apartment a sense of home was right there, an immediate hit to my sense of comfort and relaxation.

I liked where her couch sat. I liked the coffee table just in front of it and the bookshelves on the wall next to it and the raised windows behind it. I liked walking through her living room and into her kitchen, where the lighting was softer and became cozier. I liked the look of her bedroom, offset from the rest of the apartment but certainly *private*—a space that seemed like a lovely kind of fort to wake up in, isolated from the rest of the apartment and a space just right for quiet time, kissing time, laughing time, burrowing time. Perhaps I've imagined all of this because these are the things we imagine when we want a sort of life with someone—when we imagine waking up in their bed instead of our own and fixing breakfast in their kitchen and reading books on their couch.

My imagination doesn't just run wild here because I liked her; my imagination runs wild in many, if not most, of my friends' apartments when they feel homier than mine. I imagine where they spend their cozy mornings or where they go to cry or where they have sex. I imagine that they explore the space of their home in ways I can't, because all the furniture I own is confined to my bedroom and I am therefore usually confined to my bedroom, and I don't find myself spending my mornings, crying, or having sex anywhere else.

Is this a kind of development? Is my need for a "nice" home at my age the result of feeling underdeveloped in comparison to my friends? Because I haven't built anything comfortable or homey with anyone. And here's the crux: that *building* and *with* that I haven't been able to do because I've been single and confined— have I begun to have a more developed idea of what I define as home? Homes are *built*—and, surely, often by single people— but has my idea of a nice home been constructed by what I've perceived to have been built when I've seen these homes? When I can't see how a home has grown and has been maintained, I'm put off, and I judge the home as being a lesser one because I can't see or guess its history. With my own homes, or the homes of friends or family or the people I like, my comfort has lain only in guessing its history.

There's a portrait of my mother as a teenager hanging up on a wall in the basement of my grandparents' home in Waukegan. Whenever I've thought about their home I go to this image before I think about their yard or their kitchen or the bed I slept it when

I'd visit. I think I do this because the portrait makes me imagine all the years between my mother's being a teenager and her having me, and a reminder that she was once very young makes me imagine where she, in her own childhood home, liked to sit and read or where she played with her brothers and sisters or where she went to be alone whenever she needed to cry.

In Geraldyne's old house, I never imagined. I don't really know how long, before my birth, she lived in that house, but I've never been concerned with imagining my father playing there as a boy. Not just because he didn't, because he'd moved out on his own by the time she took that house, but I've also never been concerned because, although I could imagine, I was too picky about the house's cleanliness or my family being crowded into a small space with no real yard to play in. Because *I* could not be a child there, it was quite possible I didn't want to imagine that *anyone* could have had a childhood there.

My parents never moved back north after meeting in college and starting a family, simply because they didn't want to. I used to question why we had to be the ones to live outside the Chicagoland area, and my questioning made me think that maybe my parents and I share some linked ideation of home—that my parents raised us where they raised us because they wanted us to be children who played outdoors.

Here I'm imagining things again. Perhaps I prefer to. Interrogating my parents about why we were raised where we were would only take the magic away from my hometown, that magic that anyone's hometown has because it's where they first defined *home*. So for now, I'll cling to portraits. And I'll cling to the idea that we build our homes out of our sense of comfort and warmth, our sense of overall safety. And I'll cling, for now, to the hope that my idea of home will mature as I do—and that, after years of new cabinets and countertops and sinks, their sheen will matter less than knowing that they are, over anything else, mine.

TWO CITIES

The scene was Wicker Park. Years ago I lived in a more than decent apartment in this Chicago neighborhood. It had an open living room and dining room. A bedroom at each end of the unit. A pantry. Clean and lustrous hardwood floors. A kitchen for cooking. It was near the corner of Wicker Park and Evergreen avenues, and if not for the mission across the street I could've seen the actual park from my living-room window.

I lived there with two young women, Lisa and Kristy—although during my time there it was mostly just Lisa and I because Kristy had left for London to study abroad. When I'd come home from class or from work Lisa would sometimes be home alone studying or cooking, and she'd hug me as soon as I walked through the door and ask about my day. Other times she'd be with her boyfriend or in the living room with a friend or a few learning to play a new song on her ukulele. Sometimes we'd all read poetry together. Sometimes I drank a lot of wine. I was twenty-two in that apartment, and although it took the three of us to afford the place (Kristy left her rent checks behind), being just across the street from a park filled with dogs, children, and other buildings with gorgeous façades, I felt I'd reached a certain geographic success. I can remember only one neighbor around our age, who was probably also a student, and who possibly also got help affording his place.

I used to wonder whether our apartment was a preview of future cohabitation. I used to think it taught me how to cohabit—though I now know that I cannot cohabit—because it was myself, a young woman, and a gorgeous space all to ourselves. To a degree the apartment did make me feel successful. But what I actually learned here, I think, was how to exist in a neighborhood as someone young and blooming, as someone attempting to build a beautiful home. I learned how to be part of a neighborhood that was *changing*, a neighborhood I've been told used to be so different and so much worse. Now yuppies were arriving in the neighborhood, and new families who, along with a few chain businesses moving in on local stores and restaurants, helped to change the face of Wicker Park into something hipper and better for people who wanted to play. Of all the neighborhoods in Chicago Wicker Park was my favorite playground, and I aided its change by being its resident—by living in my cozy apartment and buying my clothes down the street from where I lived, by eating at cafés around the corner, by drinking at bars I could stumble home from safely. I helped make the neighborhood what it has now become, and though I didn't realize it at the time, my being a part of the neighborhood's transformation was also the illusion of my escape.

Any story I tell about my time in Chicago is a tale of two cities. One is my family's city: far south, decrepit, and colored. The other is my friends' city: safe, prosperous, and washed with white. Although I grew up in central rural Illinois, as a child I knew only my family's city, a city in which I could never play, a lacerating city filled with ubiquitous hints that not all who lived there would actually survive. I sought a different city when I moved to Chicago for college, first living in the South Loop neighborhood, then hopping around over the next near decade. I found neighborhoods where I could drink beer on sidewalk patios with friends, walk around without worrying about wearing my headphones, trade smiles with polite families passing by.

The neighborhoods I saw when visiting my relatives harbored dying buildings and rusty cars, empty lots and gated storefronts.

The city itself looked as if it couldn't *trust*, as if everything needed to be protected from barreling crime. By contrast, the neighborhoods I came to know as an adult resident of Chicago were open and clean, polished to keep the commerce coming through, no matter the day.

I spent most of my life in the city avoiding my family's neighborhoods, avoiding my family, taking only a handful of trips far south enough to spend an afternoon with a cousin or spend the night at an aunt's. And on these trips I was rarely alone, making excuses for the trips themselves as the result of yet another relative being in town—a "we should see ____ while you're here"— showing just enough thoughtfulness to keep myself off the hook. I was always too *busy*, I contended, to make trips that, even within the city, might take a couple of hours just one way.

In truth, I didn't like remembering.

I didn't like to remember visiting my family and being on edge, going to houses that reminded me of my extended family's poverty and that sat behind sidewalks that were dangerous for me to be on when I was a boy. I didn't like to remember learning about *traffic*, something I rarely encountered because my childhood home was in the woods, in a place where we children spent as much time in the street as in our yards. I didn't like to remember that the fictional violence I'd seen on TV became a possibility in front of my grandmother's house. Or my great-grandmother's. Or an uncle's or an aunt's. College gave me the feeling that I could forget what I'd known about the city and reinvent my knowledge anew. Having my own money, having white friends, having access to the city's trains and therefore access to the city allowed me to neglect—I neglected memory, neglected suspicion, neglected anything that had told me while growing up that Chicago was not a place I should be. I neglected family, and in doing so I created a new city for myself, one where I felt safe enough to make all the mistakes I felt twenty-two-year-olds should be allowed to make: partying far from home instead of in nearby spaces, sleeping on a whim at another's apartment instead of my own, being raucous in play among loud city horns and under bright city lights.

A couple summers ago, at a family reunion in Michigan, I stood in a relative's front yard while talking with my father and his uncle. We all had a beer in our hands, the scent of grilled burgers and hot dogs lingering nearby. "So," my father had asked me, "did the Mexicans move into your neighborhood yet?"

"No," I said. "I moved into theirs."

My father and his uncle burst open with their laughter. I now think it was a dismal laughter, a moment of understanding that I couldn't—and I'm bearing with myself here—*afford* to live in a neighborhood that wasn't Latinx. I'd lived too far north for my neighborhood to be mostly black, too far south for me to see white everywhere. The city of Chicago is intensely segregated by race and economic status, and although I'm black, I found myself living mostly in Latinx neighborhoods, like many other students who departed from campus dorms but couldn't afford to live around yuppies.

I wasn't in Wicker Park during the time of this picnic but in Logan Square, where I moved a couple years later and lived for over four years, and where I moved to primarily for cheaper rent. But something else, something pleasant happened when I got to this neighborhood: I found a lot of green. In college I'd heard about so many of my classmates moving to Logan for the rent and cheap bars—which was something I'd taken advantage of, surely—but no one ever told me how pretty the neighborhood was. There's a tiny park there called Palmer Square, where people run and play soccer and throw Frisbees and walk between trees on tightropes and play with their dogs and children, and the last three apartments I inhabited in Chicago were on this very square.

I'd fallen in love. I'd relished the fact that, even while still with roommates, on a graduate student income I was able to afford a place so pretty.

Things were a little different in Wicker Park. There Lisa and I ate mostly at home; we weren't frequenting the bars around our apartment and went out only sparingly, and we *played* only in ways that allowed us to spend as little money as possible. I played in Wicker less than I played in Logan, not just because I wasn't much of a drinker then but because Wicker overall felt too yuppified for me to feel like I deserved to play there. I felt, as a poor undergraduate, that I didn't belong. I'd cheated my way into the neighborhood.

When I did go out, I found myself at either the Earwax Café, whose space is now home to a Doc Martens store, or Myopic Books, where I didn't mind spending a few dollars on a nice used book. Sometimes I'd find myself at Nick's Beer Garden, a bar with a glorious shot-and-beer special five nights a week. I didn't shop often, and I wasn't as nicely dressed as my neighbors; in this respect I never even tried to fit in with them. Not that I could've succeeded in the first place.

I grew up with nice things and I therefore didn't covet them as much as nice places. I specifically coveted homes, constantly trying to figure out what counted as a nice home, what *made* a nice home. This has become more apparent as I've gotten older, living with this roommate or that one who wants a nicer TV, nicer countertops, or the convenience of an in-unit washer and dryer. These things *are* nice and convenient, but I never felt needy for them.

For as long as I can remember, though, no matter the city and no matter the continent, I've been awed when walking or driving through pretty neighborhoods and past pretty houses, and I've imagined what it might be like to inhabit them. I've coveted settings replete with trees, with tiny brick houses and fake log cabins, and it's likely that I've coveted these settings because I myself have been geographically spoiled. I've always—and here's a hint of my privilege—had trees at which to stare or on which to climb, enough food to eat, heating and cooling, and plenty of electronic entertainment. But since I left my parents I've found I've drifted from many of the things so readily available to me when I was with them, and I've gotten picky about what I want to see when I exit my front door.

Whenever we left Wicker Park to visit our families, Lisa and I had yet another part of the city in common. Her parents lived off the Thirty-Fifth Street train stop, the same stop I got off when visiting an aunt and uncle. I was most familiar with Thirty-Fifth from having gone with Lisa to her parents' house, because it was a rarer thing for me to visit my aunt and uncle. I only really saw them when my cousin Gabrielle was in town from college in Wisconsin; I'd take the train down to see her, and maybe her brother too. She was my best friend in high school, made possible by our phones and by our daily AOL messenger chats, so we did our best when we got to college to speak just as often and as openly as we had when going through our high school dramas.

The Thirty-Fifth Street stop is just after Chinatown, which was where our college orientation leaders and dormitory RAs told us never to venture beyond. When riding the train, you'd notice that it was also where well-dressed white passengers started getting off and were replaced by minorities, drunk passengers, and homeless riders who used the train for its warmth. Our RAs told us that after Chinatown the city starts becoming unsafe. I wonder, now that I'm a little older, if their message was just a coded warning about its being less white.

I never liked going to Thirty-Fifth, to be honest, but everything was made more bearable by Lisa's or Gabi's presence. It wasn't actually all that out of the way, but I didn't like that I had to enter a different mode of being in the city whenever I was there. I didn't like that every stranger who approached me was a possible threat. I didn't like that I couldn't tune the world out with my headphones but instead had to listen for arguments in case they became something more. And I didn't like that, while Lisa's house was a "safe" walking distance from the train, my family had me wait at the station and picked me up by car. I would've preferred a walk.

Nine times out of ten when Gabi came to visit we'd meet farther north and she'd stay at my dorm. This way I could justify never leaving my comfort zone, especially because she'd started to become friends with my college friends and roommates, and we could surround ourselves with more than just her parents. I never told her, but my not wanting to go to her parents' house was tied to my perception of the South Loop as a safer space; whether Thirty-Fifth was really all that bad or not didn't matter because my reaction to the city as stimulus was what got me to think and act the way I did. It's the same, I realize now, as my RA's advice about the city, the same as many who never left their own neighborhoods because they'd accepted the city's cultivation of fear.

I can understand my own hesitancy when I'm traveling—in a place like Prague, where by avoiding certain parts of the city I also avoid its Nazis. I can understand it when I visit New York, because I'm a stranger there and at a total loss for navigation, sticking around my friends' apartments and populated tourist sites. I even understand it in Paris, where my belonging—really, my safety—might be a matter of my lack of religious garb and the giving away of my Americanness, and the places in the city I know to avoid are the places many Americans will avoid.

But I cannot understand my hesitancy in Chicago, a place where my feet first hit pavement every year of my life and then eventually every day of my years in the city, and where it would make the most sense for my living there to be chameleonic, for me to switch between a hard, impolite, and self-preserving Southside self and a warm, approachable, and well-dressed yuppie. I do not know how I managed only one *real* mode—the other modes actually false because they were just different shades of suspicion—or how I managed to so easily disregard others who inhabited modes different from my own.

I'm often brought to consider my geographic pickiness when I walk through Wicker Park these days. And while I'm thinking about pickiness—my own as well as that of the shoppers and residents around me—I also see an inverted kind of pickiness, that of Wicker's newest, and temporary, inhabitants. I've heard them called many names: "crust punks," "gutter punks," "road kids," "oogles," and "crusties." They're twenty-somethings who've chosen to live in "voluntary poverty" and are "selectively home-less," traveling through numerous cities by freight train to avoid having to work for The Man. They often bring their dogs with them, and they're dirty and scruffy and willing to panhandle ("spinge" is their word) for anything that passersby are willing to give. They reappear in Wicker whenever it begins to get warm again, and only while it's warm, coming around year after year for a new spinging season.

I'm perplexed by them and by their situation(s). Of course there's an obvious social problem of a poverty that can be turned on and off, of a pickiness that can lead someone either into a home or into a gutter. But how do they decide where to make themselves at home, I wonder. How does one decide where to squat? Where to be at home for a few weeks or months before moving on or going back to what they had before?

"We travel for fun," says twenty-five-year-old Devlyn, in Alisa Hauser's *DNAinfo Chicago* feature "Traveling 'Gutter Punk' Home-less Back in City," "to do something other than wake up in the exact same place every day to go to the exact same job and see the exact same people and do the exact same things at exactly the same time." It would be easy to call them foolish, stupid. And maybe they are. Maybe some of them have worried parents back home who shake their heads, waiting for their children to return to good sense and productive citizenship. Others, I've heard, travel for more dismal reasons, like having drug-addicted or abusive parents, making it complicated to generalize (though isn't it always?) about the group as a whole.

What I try to see when I look at them is a reason for sympathy rather than pity, a reason to feel the weight of homelessness and make myself want to act on it, reinforcing my own sense of privilege. Even as a child, as the ringleader of the few children who lived in my neighborhood, I'd convince them to join me in packing bags and lunch boxes, then walking with me into the woods to pretend we were runaways. The dangers of the wildlife or even the other human beings we might have encountered wasn't totally lost on us. We wanted adventure, and we found it by giving up the safety of our home lives.

Both of my grandmothers would certainly call the road kids idiots. I've heard my parents' growing-up stories about using ovens as space heaters, picking dandelion greens from a nearby field to eat, and using leftover rice as cereal. My family members would agree, probably in unison, that class is not operable by a light switch. The road kids might say otherwise. Just how much privilege does it take, I wonder, for those who left comfy homes to make new ones three cars from a caboose and plop down in Wicker Park for a few weeks? Do I enact the same kind of privilege working in the other direction when, in front of the mirror, I button my shirt and remind myself of the palpable class distance between two generations?

I started to read Jack Kerouac when I entered my twenties; he made my friends and me think that we could leave everything we had and pack our bags into my Jeep and live in interstate freedom. There was something romantic and selfish about this idea, which would've had our parents worried sick had we enacted it, but we still spent plenty of time thinking about where to go, what we'd do when we got there, how to work under the table to prep for our next little run at things.

I'm guilty, like the road kids, of having romanticized the notion of homelessness here—of trying to give it more pathos—which makes me think that had I actually vagabonded myself (as I wanted to do when I read Kerouac) like they're doing now, I wouldn't have earned or deserved any pity. My homelessness wouldn't have been real, a safety net always still hanging in a house across the street from a corn field in central Illinois, my position fostered by a youthful need to escape class position in a downward direction. But it's the *upward* movement I should've been thinking about—in reflection of every earned and accumulated paycheck since my birth—so that I can never forget that, in reality, it's only those up high who get to do the pitying.

One of the first things that excited me about my move to Wicker Park was that it was a neighborhood in which I thought I could better fit in than where I'd been before. I'd been in the Lincoln Park neighborhood just prior, where I lived around the corner from a Starbucks, an Einstein Bros. Bagels, and a high-rise with a rooftop pool. If belonging in a neighborhood meant having money, then I'd faked every moment of my time in Lincoln Park by living in a place where I could barely afford the rent and certainly couldn't afford to play close to home.

When I got to Wicker I was elated to be more able to join my friends at restaurants and bars, to shop for books, to carry my clothes to the laundromat just like everybody else. We found camaraderie in our age and status, laughing our way not to the bank but to the bar, and though it could be said Wicker Park held four kinds of people (college students, yuppies, hipsters, and road kids), we all, even in contradiction, belonged there together. And sometimes, when out to play, we found an unfortunate clash between our categories. Belonging, I would have to learn, needed to be about more than just money.

I used to own an inexpensive black winter jacket that I got at Target, which I wore when it wasn't cold enough for gloves or a real winter coat. It looked a little big on me—would've looked a little big on anyone my height. It was made of more cotton than necessary. It never would've been my favorite jacket, but it did the trick when Chicago's weather didn't batter my body.

One winter night I agreed to meet friends at Nick's Beer Garden. I put on my jacket and walked around the neighborhood, first making a pit stop at Myopic Books to browse their new acquisitions, which I did most weekend nights, before walking the rest of the way down the street until I got to Nick's. My friends were sitting in a back room, a synthetic indoor garden kept warm in the winter. In the summer it was a nice little space between the sun and the indoor breeze.

I sat with them, going to their table first instead of to the bar. Though I knew I'd probably be starting my night with Blue Moon I wanted to pretend to think about what else I might drink. But before I could order, before I could stand again after sitting, two police officers entered the back room of the bar, walked over to our table, and asked if they could have a word with me outside. Sure, I said. Sure.

They had a squad car parked out back, just behind the bar, sitting on gravel beneath tracks that roared whenever a train went by. They asked that I place my hands on the trunk as they patted me down and searched me, looking through my wallet and asking questions about who I was. "Is this the correct address on your license?" No. "What are you up to tonight?" Just drinking with some friends. This and that, et cetera. After a few minutes they told me I could take my hands off the car, gave me back my wallet, and said I could go back inside. "We're really sorry about that," one officer said. "It's just that you fit the description of a guy we're looking for." I know I responded politely, though I don't know what I said, but knowing myself it was probably, "Sure thing!" or, "No problem!" But whatever voice escaped in my response, it wasn't the voice matching the one in my head—the voice in my head wasn't my own, wasn't even one I knew, but it crept slowly toward my ear and whispered one single word: *Remember*.

I did as I was told and went back inside, sitting with my friends and returning to thoughts of Blue Moon. Then a tall one appeared right in front of me, the bartender walking over and delivering it himself. "It's on the house," he said. "We're so sorry that happened." My friends and I drank, certainly to excess, eventually leaving behind our thoughts of how the night had started. I made it home, eventually, probably stumbling and shivering at once, miraculously never taking a fall on the icy sidewalk. When I entered my apartment I breathed in its warm air, and not a second later threw my jacket in the trash.

Although I didn't have a designer dog to take to the dog-grooming shop Wicker Bark, nor an infant to push around in a stroller, or even a route in the neighborhood on which to jog every morning, I kept a desire in Wicker Park to preserve the pretty interior of my apartment and to enjoy the view from my living room's bay window. I desired to have a place replete with coziness over convenience. I wanted (and still want) a grandmotherly kind of home sitting unnoticed in a quiet, tree-filled neighborhood.

It has always been strange for me when I try to define home, its meaning wavering somewhere between trying to *decide* on a home and trying to *build* a home out of safety and fond memories. As a concept it's tied to notions of my loyalty to place, because while home may be for some (like me) a place latched onto dreams, for others it's congruent with nativity, congruent with nostalgia. The way I remember places where I've visited and lived, I realize that I attempted to leave these places with too hasty an escape. My own nostalgia makes me form comfort where I can absorb the memories of the places themselves so that I can look back on them one day, eventually making the place a part of who I've become.

No matter where I've lived in Chicago, I know now that I must remember. Must remember that while my neighborhoods have shown me how close I've come to getting what I want, they've also shown me how I've been marked, how belonging might mean showing my bruises to others who've also been wounded by the city.

Today is July 4, and I write from my parents' house. It's the first Independence Day I've had in the United States in three years, and all around I see people at home preparing for cookouts and daytime drinking. Their neighbors are mowing their lawns, washing off their patio furniture, wheeling out the coolers to fill them with ice. And while the independence of any nation should be celebrated, some of these neighbors are doing the same things they'd be doing on any old Saturday afternoon in the summer, celebrating a day of leisure.

There should be something definable about our homes, whether we live in houses with yards and fences or in towering apartments with balconies. Maybe when I've finally built a home of my own I *will* have one like my grandmother's, where I tell people where everything safely belongs, and where no matter how fussy I've become in my old age I'll smile inside because I'll have finally found a place I have no desire to flee.

PLAYGROUND CITY

During my final semester of college, I went into work one day at a campus computer lab perched up on a mezzanine, over an open space and stage down below—all that green and all that gray, and everything enveloped by it, never got a second look from me. But on this day the college held an orientation for new students, and the orientation leaders, college students themselves, took the stage for informal introductions. I paid attention to only one of these students.

There are moments when we ask for the names of those who hold our sight, a whispered *Who are you?* and a slow step forward—or, in my case, a lean. I would've fallen had glass not held me up. And although I did not fall, there was the drop of my stomach and my breath.

The word "curious" is too mild. I was a *captive*, the way one is held by a photograph, a painting, a film.

I saw her for days after this, as orientation went on throughout the week, and every day I was captive. When orientation ended I thought of the ways things can skirt, can come close without touching—and then, with a blink, disappear into memory.

She was sitting at my workstation the next time I entered the lab, and I felt that drop again. We were introduced. "Micah." "Miranda. How do you do?" she said. My secret: I'd been watching for days, and now she was here and she knew that I too existed. An embarrassing secret, one that had me flush out of fear of being found out.

Weeks later Miranda and I found ourselves together in bookstores, by Lake Michigan getting coffee or a burger, a movie, a drink. On the night of that winter's first snow we found ourselves in Chicago's Old Town neighborhood on the corner of North and Wells, where two black, steel arches that stretched across the street invited us to play. The end of that night had me giddy— soft snowflakes landing on our lashes, sipping hot cocoa on the train after waving goodbye.

Because of what I came to learn about her past I found Miranda sincere—I found her good, and filled with kindness and bravery and that, above all, she tried her very best. This felt like the discovery of a "special someone," and I held my cocoa close to subdue my bliss, to keep the image of myself unwanting.

I sipped my cocoa in distraction, looking out at the city lights from a fast-moving train car. All that light, in winter, seemed to creep through the cold air and was somehow comforting.

I had begun something important here, I realized. I had begun to play. In this city, which before was so looming, frightening, intimidating (I was intimidated; I felt suffocated by the city's height and size), through play with Miranda I was learning to ease up. Learning to relax my shoulders and smile at things I hadn't noticed before. I didn't know it at the time, but I was falling in love, both in and with the city.

I once remarked during a walk down State Street with a friend that I thought it would be strange to be a teenager living in the city because there's so much here to play with. There are buses and trains to ride in reckless fashion. There are parts of the city, State Street and Michigan Avenue, that act as a shopping center, more like malls than roads to a destination. There's Navy Pier. The Sears Tower Skydeck. Beaches bursting with Frisbee throwers and dog walkers.

When I thought about all of this I thought of my hometown in central Illinois, where my geography was limited to wherever my legs or bike could carry me. I rode past cornfields, to friends' houses, to the soccer field for solitary practice, around the track behind my junior high school, over mounds of dirt at construction sites, through the quads of local universities.

For the most part I was a solitary child and teenager, pedaling past those parts of town that felt like freedom because they weren't as lonely as my bedroom, which was littered with toys and whatever else I had lying around. Asking myself now to remember what I kept in my bedroom as a child has me trying not to fill my memory with some imaginary happiness when there was loneliness and solid rejection.

I can't imagine who I would have become had I grown up in Chicago, but I do imagine the ways I might've played here. The way I see children and teenagers play here now, not needing bikes to escape because they have their trains or their skateboards or their buses, knowing they can look up and see glass and metal instead of sky. I imagine I would've played like them. I would have been loud, would have been made jubilant by the rush of the city, and, I'm sure, I would've been troublesome. But isn't this sometimes how nostalgia works? Can't it have us imagine happiness in the places where we could've been?

As roaming children we never got caught doing the things we did. No one knew that the emergency buttons on security checkpoints around campus were pushed by my friends and me just before we sped away on our bikes, before campus security could catch us. No one caught our faces after the drops of our spit fell from rooftops and bridges because we hid, and, when the roof was low enough, we jumped off and ran away to put ourselves in the clear. My friends and I amused ourselves when our town didn't give us enough to do—especially before we could drive (and when we *could* drive, we drag-raced and did doughnuts in parking lots), seeking the thrills bored rural children and teenagers seek.

What I remember most about play in my hometown is that when it wasn't solitary it was dangerous. At age seven or eight my friends and I pretended to run away from home by packing our bags with lunches and sneaking off into the nearby woods. When we were fifteen we would jump with our bikes or Rollerblades off the most daring heights we could find. At seventeen we raced cars through deserted streets late at night. And at nineteen some of us partied on a friend's farm while we watched furniture burn in grass that was dangerously close to corn.

Play for a child is an exercise in risk, and though my imaginary youth in Chicago is far different from my actual youth, I admit here to imagining only one kind of urban childhood and adolescence: the kind tied to danger. I've imagined that the risk of getting caught in front of hundreds of people, instead of just a few or a dozen, would have fueled more within me than a trembling hatchback at 80 mph ever could.

Miranda and I had made dinner plans one night, but when I learned that the restaurant we wanted to go to would close before she got off work, I brought her a white hot chocolate from Dunkin' Donuts instead. I saw her working in the lab; my stomach dropped (as always with Miranda); and I put the drink on the counter next to her things while I thought up a plan.

"Well," she said to me, "what would you suggest we do instead?"

"I thought of two things," I said. "One is that there's a movie playing at 10:45 over at River East, and the other is that we can just go back to my place and heat up some bread and drink some wine with it while we listen to music." I hoped for the latter. There was a bottle of Saint-Émilion I'd brought back from a recent trip to Paris that was waiting for her company, and I wanted to show her what I drank with breakfast every morning during my trip.

I also wanted music, because Miranda loved music more than anyone I'd ever known; she kept a library of it in her head, could spout lyrics and tunes at the drop of a hat and without shame, and this was part of what I was falling for. I always felt understudied compared to her, didn't have a list of bands I loved or lyrics I kept inside my heart, and I thought it marvelous that she was my opposite in this way. It was one of the many things about her that impressed me.

Because of her I started going to live shows in the city—shows in dark rooms, with bodies squeezed in like sardines and moving lights shining down from the ceiling. My fervor for music had never gone beyond my stereo or my headphones, but after meeting Miranda I learned to bob my head to live sound and, with her, dance without shyness. The music would play and we would dance and I'd learn to be unafraid of this. I would learn, because of her, how not to be shy about the sounds I loved.

We decided on the music. And the wine and bread with Camembert, which I'd also brought back from Paris. We talked, ate, drank, listened, and sang along when we knew the words. I played her music by Ray LaMontagne and Dear and the Headlights— an artist and a band I loved because she gave me their albums. I wanted their songs to be *our* songs, the way my parents and I had songs, the way my parents had songs with each other, the way I had songs with ex-lovers and best friends and my little sister. I wanted songs that we could share in secret, could grasp in memory to bring the other person to mind. I wanted Miranda stuck in my head when I heard them.

When we were children my little sister and I were charged with cleaning the house on days when we didn't go to school but our parents had to work. We'd wipe down the cabinets and polish the railings and wash the mirrors and windows as we played music as loud as we could on my father's impressive stereo system, music from the boy bands we'd bonded over and learned the words and sometimes choreography to when they danced in music videos. Though I owned cassettes all through elementary school I got my first CD player for my thirteenth birthday, and my first CD was the debut album by the boy band *NSYNC.

Miranda needed to get home by midnight. We bundled up for the cold, and in a moment of play by my front door we stole each other's hats and scarves, then posed as each other as we walked to the train, arm-in-arm during some moments, waddling like penguins in others. In front of the turnstiles at the station, we re-traded our hats and scarves, and I rested my forehead against hers, my hat placed sillily between our faces, an imaginary barrier to keep the moment from getting serious.

"Goodnight, Micah," she said, then slipped her arms under mine and around my back for a hug that lasted longer than expected. It was a hug that filled me, that made me feel I'd done things right that night, and then seconds later I watched her go through the turnstile. She told me to be good and I said, "You too," and we said goodnight again before she walked out of sight.

Please let me know when you get home safe, I texted.

I just made it in the door. Night night, she texted back an hour later.

That was it for me. I decided that I loved her—decided that, at the rate we were going, it would be impossible not to. She wasn't one I could just *like*—with time and with more play, my heels would be in the air.

The first time I was happy about the sight of the city was from a plane that had just crossed the Atlantic. When it descended low enough it gave me an image of Chicago's skyscrapers that made me utter the word "home" for the first time since I'd moved here. It took me leaving the country and returning to be glad to see this place.

I want to put a twist here on Roland Barthes's beloved word *jouissance*, making it instead a *jouessance*, from "play" and "joy"— *jouessance* as a pure and simple enjoyment of play. *Jouessance* is what we feel as we grow, as we learn to explore our states (of mind, of geography) and come to terms with the worlds around and within us. It's the flourishing feeling that comes with an ability to make others laugh and swoon.

"The Festivity is what is waited for," Barthes writes in *A Lover's Discourse*, "what is expected. What I expect of the promised presence is an unheard-of totality of pleasures, a banquet; I rejoice like the child laughing at the sight of the mother whose mere presence heralds and signifies a plenitude of satisfactions: I am about to have before me, and for myself, the 'source of all good things.'" In this city Festivity is what youth craves. Youth craves a banquet, a totality of pleasures, a plenitude of satisfactions. Youth craves the touch of another, slipping into incoherence, the slipping of the tongue (especially against another), slipping into sleep after a night of pure joy.

There's no excuse for what my own youth has done with the city. Except for, maybe, youth. And my youth has craved its share of company here: sober, drunk, garrulous, wet, naked. It has craved long nights filled with bare skin and long walks and philosophy. It has craved the loss of memory, of dexterity, and the ignorance of weight and sadness. The state of my youth has had to shed so much here, but in shedding there has always been a trade: my own stories for yours, my skin for your skin, my thoughts for your thoughts, my laughter for your laughter.

The joy of youth lies in sharing. At first we share toys, and then we share secrets and skin. These ways of sharing and play, all new for me, helped me grow in the city; they made me comfortable, made me challenge the city, made me reach for all of its good things.

Sitting just next to play is love, for even a child who plays wants to do so with care. My wanting to reach out, to share and trade, has been with those I've brought close. The expressions of my desire to play have always been from a high regard—from looking and then, later, a wish to move closer, a wish to care. I've been no different with the city than with its people.

The day before I left for Paris, Miranda and I met for a boat tour put on by the Chicago Architecture Foundation. I'd booked our tickets days prior, both excited and terrified by my own romantic gesture.

We rode up and down the river, and the buildings towered over us—spires and columns and reflective panes of glass all hovered above from a view of the city I'd never taken in before and that shaped new feelings for the city I'd never felt before.

I wore leather gloves that didn't fit because my hands are small, much like Miranda's, though her gloves were made of black cotton and they fit her hands perfectly. I wondered throughout our ride whether her hands were too cold, and for the first time I thought to reach out for them—I thought of holding one of them with one of mine while our other hands held our cocoa. It might've distracted us from the towering glass.

"A squeeze from the hand—," Barthes writes, "enormous documentation—a tiny gesture within the palm, a knee which doesn't move away, an arm extended, as if quite naturally, along the back of a sofa and against the other's head gradually comes to rest—this is the paradisiac realm of subtle and clandestine signs: a kind of festival not of the senses but of meaning." I imagined holding Miranda's hand for warmth and to feel that festival of meaning. I imagined her small hand pressed against mine, thin cotton against thick leather, fingers fitting into one another while our covered hands met palm to palm.

I didn't take her hand. I was afraid—afraid of her hand's rejection of my own, which would then be left on my knee or in my pocket, buried inside my glove and safe from the coldness of that distance made by her hand moving away. Instead I watched her face: she viewed the buildings in wide-eyed amazement, something about her gaze open to marvel and wonder, and something about my gaze open to hers.

After the tour, at sundown, we found our way through a crowd watching the Festival of Lights. When we crossed the bridge on Michigan, too much risk of losing each other, *she* took *my* hand and pulled me forward, and we squeezed ourselves past bouncing bodies.

We were stuck. I looked west, to my left, out at a slithering river and the buildings reflected in it. Then, in one impeccable moment, Chicago became very real to me: the river cut through the city of majesty it mirrored; I found a favorite spot in this place; and I finally felt the smallness of Miranda's hand, the softness of her glove pressed against mine. It was my moment of no longer being afraid.

"The gift is a contact," Barthes writes, "sensuality: you will be touching what I have touched, a third skin unites us." A fourth skin, in our case: her glove had touched mine, and this was the *gift*. The gloves covered our hands, our first skins, and their coming together ignited within me the wish to begin giving back (to this woman, to this city)—to this place that had become so real and so clear.

We later ended up far north in the city, looking for a sweater and a peacoat. I'd wanted to look "appropriate" for Paris, and we first searched a store downtown and then two more stores up north. We tried on different clothes, played dress-up. Miranda was fickle about all the things she wore. When she asked for my thoughts, no matter what she was wearing, I always thought she was lovely.

"The love story," according to Barthes, "(the 'episode', the 'adventure') is the tribute the lover must pay to the world in order to be reconciled with it." Because I've come to recognize this bridge between play and love, have I paid a worthy tribute? Have I now reconciled with a city that gave me both?

My love for the city germinated through play with Miranda. And though I'd planned to leave this place, was happy to abandon it, my little sister moved here on a whim and needed me to stay (or so I'd convinced myself). Had I left, I thought I would've felt my mother's rage and disappointment, brought on by my deserting a beloved sibling. What I admit only now, though, is that I also stayed for play. I stayed for a growing love of a place, brought on by a sudden love for a person.

The first time I wanted to utter an *I love you* to Miranda was months after our boat ride, on the night of our graduation party. I didn't utter it (why didn't I utter it?) but instead soaked in the scene of our walking down Michigan Avenue, streetlights shining in mid-May, the winter having ended, and cocoa far from our thoughts.

When a taxi pulled up to the curb, I hugged her and said *I love you* in my head, eyes closed tight to hold in the regret of silence. She got in the cab, closed the door, gave the driver her address, and he sped off under the streetlights into a landscape of gigantic glass and majesty. My regard, my secret, were held within me. A containment of pure bliss.

PRAGUE

SNOW GLOBE BOHEMIA

There are days when I can feel this city in my gut. Sometimes I can remember a very specific street corner or the inside of a café. I have plenty of dreams about Prague too, when I'm lost in the throes of topography and language. Dreams when I'm revisiting streets I've walked a dozen times or when I'm speaking fluent Czech to friends and strangers, although in reality I do not speak fluent Czech.

These are obsessive dreams, I realize—they're dreams in which I'm remembering streets, imagining bars that don't exist, even being there with friends who've never set foot in Prague before. I know these dreams are tied to imagination and not just to my memory: there's no place on Earth that pervades both memory and imagination for me more than Prague, which tells me that either I'm impressionable when it comes to certain geography or that Prague itself leaves a potent and pleasant residue. The city of Prague has left more than an imprint on me. It has left a crater.

I began dreaming about Prague years ago, after my first stint in the city, at age twenty-one. For years after returning from that first trip, I had dreams that took place here. When I studied abroad in Prague for the first time, I visited other cities and other countries, but now when I bring them up in memory they serve as mere photographs. Prague, by comparison, seems like an entire movie.

What itches is that I can't figure out why, of all the places I've seen and committed to memory, I've only really dreamed about one. It's as if the city is an old lover or a lost friend or relative, and I've adopted a nostalgia for the memories we've made together. But that's silly; Prague itself can't make memories *with me*, so the burden of nostalgia is weighted on my side. I cannot meet this city in a bar and reminisce. We cannot take a walk together and catch up on the new details of our lives. We cannot partake in anything for old times' sake.

My first suspicion is that my relationship to the city of Prague isn't like love at all, but like obsession. Parts of my own apartment are a shrine to the city: pictures and postcards from friends and from my own travels are attached to my walls; old photographs are still on my computer; and in aching moments I revisit the city on the internet just to remember it. I've told friends and family (and myself) for years how much I love Prague, but actual scrutiny of my relationship with the city has me recognizing something else.

What does it mean to obsess over a city? My initial guess is that we cling to the cities that marvel, whether or not we've set foot in them, because they help us bridge the gap between geography and romance. I can't say how many people I've met who have wanted to see Paris or London or Rome, giving little (if any) thought to the ugly parts of every locale, a clear negligence of the cities' unromantic qualities. Instead we want our cities to be beautiful, to reflect our best ideals, and we want these reflections free of any ugliness.

This is something I've attempted with my memory of Prague, though I know the city is far from a perfect one. It has its clear, visible class distinctions. Sometimes the graffiti is more serious than in the United States, displaying a swastika on the wall rather than some other "rebellious" symbol or phrase, which scares me a little as a black American. And the winters here are often overcast, a far less ideal situation than one would find when hoping for snowy but sunny days.

What was pitched to me first about Prague was a collective imagination of this city: it's an old and beautiful city, one of the least grazed by European war, and the beer and food are very cheap for a Westerner. What could be more beautiful? Ah, yes, the women! Tall and short, busty and not, Czech women are some of the most beautiful women in the world, and so very ready to throw themselves at lucky Americans. (Though this is a joke, I find some of it to be true.)

For a romantic American, conflating imagination and geography can be a dangerous thing. This isn't to say that a Parisian can't dream of one day going to New York or LA, but for an American, Europe has its own kind of romance that only we Americans seem to yearn for: a far-reaching history.

Prague was pitched strongly to me when I prepared to study there as an undergraduate, as a living artifact: people have lived here for centuries, which is an easier statement to make about a European city than any American one. Here our geographic flirtation begins: we yearn for a homecoming, knowing so many of our family lines came from other continents, and we're awed by the places built prior to constructing our own American Empire.

Perhaps this is why (and perhaps this is unfair to say), when many Europeans imagine "America," they imagine New York City. It's not only the oldest metropolis in the United States, but its portrayal in film, photography, even music can give the impression that it's the place of every American's dreams. I don't think this is wholly true, but many Europeans I've met have dreamed only of New York when they've dreamed of their America—or, if they've visited the States, New York was the only place they saw.

More than just pitting geography and romance against each other, I'm thinking here about geography and imagination—the way we can imagine a Paris or a New York, and how different the place can be from what we get when we finally touch it. Maybe this is why I think of Prague so often; when I see it in films or photographs it's filled to the brim with magic, and though this is not to say there *isn't* some magic to be found there in person, in the end I've paid just as much attention to the city's stains. Conflating these stains with the photographic or cinematic magic of the city, juxtaposing my own memory with the world's (or perhaps just a Westerner's) curiosity, is what snags me when a tiny thought of Prague enters my mind.

"The more I felt I was losing my city," Luc Sante writes of NYC in his essay "My Lost City," "the more preoccupied I became with it. I gradually became interested in its past, an interest that grew into obsession." I don't know what triggered my obsession with Prague, but I know that, like Sante, over time my mere interest transformed into something more.

The first time I studied there, my teachers encouraged us all to soak in the scenery by taking walks, taking pictures, taking one another to outdoor cafés. It was as if they *wanted* us to marvel, as if we'd been offered no other choice. The second time I studied there, however, in a Czech literature class at Charles University, I read and learned more about the city than it ever occurred to me to care about. My professor didn't care one bit about us soaking up any scenery—likely because, as a Praguer, there was nothing there for him to be novelly wowed by. He was more preoccupied with teaching us Czech history through literature's lens.

I realize, as I write this sentence, that learning Czech history was what triggered my obsession. It wasn't at all the same as, say, taking a formal tour of the Louvre in Paris or walking through the Anne Frank House in Amsterdam, because what I gained by learning history in Prague was the reenvisioning of a city I'd experienced before. Before, I had learned nothing about Vyšehrad and too much about Kafka. I was too focused on the city as a muse for writers and artists rather than as a religious, cultural, or political nucleus. What I gained during my second visit was depth, which is the central difference between interest and obsession.

As with Sante, it also took the fear of loss to inspire my obsession. I am afraid of losing this city. I'm afraid of its being defaced, I'm afraid of losing its details in memory, and because of this I've read and written about it and have visited every time I've had the money to do so. If Prague has claws, as Kafka once pronounced, then I've embraced its formidable grip, telling it to take me every time it reaches in.

It has been a kind of love affair, but not one in which the two lovers gradually fall for each other. Instead there's a dependency: when the two are separated there's a sharp, penetrative yearning, more extreme than just missing the desired person. An itch that's needing to be scratched.

I know this feeling too well, and it isn't love. It's an *I miss the way you feel* or an *I need you now*, but not an *I miss you, and I hope you're well*. This need I have to keep Prague in memory is, well, how else can we say "disease"? Malady? Canker? Affliction? Should we call it a bug that simply won't go away? I am afflicted by Prague, and I suffer when we've been apart for too long. I know this is a far from healthy love when what I'm trying to hold onto isn't the Prague that moves through time but the Prague that sits in my own vacuum, my bubble, my snow globe. What I have to reconcile within myself is that my relationship to this city is actually about my relationship to my memory of the city.

"I was in love with New York," Joan Didion writes in her essay "Goodbye to All That." "I do not mean 'love' in any colloquial way, I mean that I was in love with the city, the way you love the first person who ever touches you and you never love anyone quite that way again." Bingo. The way Didion frames her feelings about her eight years in New York evokes my own feelings about any time I've spent in Prague, and the debatable point here is which feeling is stronger between "the first person who ever touches you" and the first city that ever touches you. Both speak of a kind of virginal experience; there was a certain innocence I lost when I first came to Prague, and its touch is always there, lingering in memory. It's a contact that returns to my memory with fondness.

The notion of travel being compared to the loss of virginity is more cliché than sincere, but I suppose it depends on whether this loss remains, on whether the experience is held in memory rather than erased with the passage of time. As with stories about the loss of virginity, storytelling about travel is sometimes met with great fondness, but sometimes the story is told without a single hint of vim and vigor.

When I tell my own stories about my first visit to Prague they're sometimes halfhearted tellings, as if I instead want to jump into the future, to better times in the city, when I was older than twenty-one and made less youthful decisions here. I can remember, for instance, sitting down with my parents with a photo album after I got home the first time, giving them a backstory to every image to fill them in on the juicy details of my trip. But were I to try to do that five years later, it would feel too much like giving them an essay; the backstory for every photograph would be coupled with the reasons I took the picture, conflating a history learned with a history interpreted. Because I've learned more and more about the city every time I've visited, that first youthful visit becomes less important in memory, a detail to be neglected every time I go fishing for things I love about Prague.

"I could stay up all night and make mistakes," Didion writes, "and none of them would count." My young nights in Prague, spent with a beer or a joint in hand, waiting with friends for the sun to rise, I'd come to discover would be pushed to the back of my memory to make room for better ones—memories of certain meals, certain conversations, certain walks that I'd never want to forget—and I would come to value the new memories more than I'd value the old ones. The old ones, in the end, simply would not count.

I don't have the same relationship with Prague that many people have with their own beloved cities, because I've never stayed. I've gone to Prague five times in the past ten years, and I hope to be able to keep up this rate of contact, but unlike Didion in New York or James Baldwin or Gertrude Stein in Paris, my contact has never been a lasting one. My visits have been short affairs, and only sometimes do I wish to prolong them.

This is perhaps the best proof to me that I'm more likely obsessed with the city than in love with it. I appreciate my short bursts in the city—the mornings, days, and nights there that I know won't be repeated for months or years—that I soak up, knowing that the details of one night in the city can be clearer than details spread out over years in my relationship with it. Here's that virginal parallel again: I want to remember the one-night stand and am willing to forget the long affair.

I wear the city of Prague like a tattoo: it's been both donned and imprinted and has become, for me, my own formative and metaphorical kind of New York. "I wasn't born in New York," Sante writes, "and I may never live there again, and just thinking about it makes me melancholy, but I was changed forever by it, and my imagination is manacled to it, and I wear its mark the way you wear a scar."

ISLAND IN THE CITY

One summer when I was in Prague, I visited Vaclavské naměstí, Wenceslas Square, almost every day for the *Vaclavske klobasa*, the Wenceslas sausage. It isn't the average sausage found in Prague, which is typically served with a single slice of bread and a dipping portion of Czech mustard. This sausage is around eight or nine inches long, served in a bun an inch or two shorter than the link. You could buy it from street vendors at any one of three or four stands on the square, ordering the Menu 1 (meal number) or by saying, "Klobasa prosím," which gets you the sausage and a twenty-ounce Coke for 85 Kč, or about $4.50.

I visited one of these stands every day, but not just for the sausage. It was the Czech mustard, you see. Czech mustard is some kind of meticulous and mysterious blend of yellow and honey mustard, beautiful and impeccable proportions of both potency and sweetness hitting the palate at once; it's the best mustard I've ever had in my life.

I hope to someday bring some of this mustard back to the United States. I hope to hoard it in my baggage and store it in my fridge and use it slowly, sparingly, until it's all gone.

At these stands you can also order a Pilsner Urquell, large or larger, to go with your sausage. And they have other Coke brands as well: Diet, Sprite, Fanta. If it isn't the sausage you want you can eat the *bramboračky* (potato pancakes) or the Czech favorite: fried cheese as a mozzarella patty, sometimes naked, sometimes on a bun. It's the Czechs' most popular food, in all its fried, stringy, artery-clogging eloquence.

A professor of mine at Charles University once told my class about the particulars of Czech dining—that 65 percent of the four to six million tourists who visit Prague every year say beer is their first motivation for visiting, that even the locals choose restaurants at which to dine based on beer price, and that, if you're a good Czech, you don't eat for the nutrition. You eat to enjoy the taste of the food and to get fat around the belly.

To enjoy a meal without counting its calories is to be a good Czech. To get fat around the belly means you've enjoyed a meal, and therefore life, and this also makes one a good Czech. "The fatter the better," my professor would say, to give a meal its merits. And it wasn't that Czechs were just discounting nutrition or enjoying a hedonistic life. They want a belly, he'd say, in order to be prepared for any future famine and despair.

In Prague one winter I found that many of the vendors on Vaclavské náměstí had closed for the season, including the one or two regular vendors I visited for my *klobasa* the previous summer. In the summer, this was my most Czech ritual: visiting a vendor while being prepared to pay for food with little to no nutritional value, only because it's an easy and enjoyable meal. It was easy to buy the *klobasa* and Pilsner, then grab a bench and eat as I watched the pedestrian traffic pass by.

In winter, though, I can't lounge. The cold is too sharp for that. There are little stands in the square for shelter, little silver towers with roofs overhead to guard from falling rain or snow, but they're unheated. I remove my gloves to hold the sausage, and it doesn't take much time for my fingers to lose their dexterity in the prickling cold. Because of this there's no time for beer, and I settle for a Fanta instead because at least I can put the cap back on the bottle when I'm finished eating, place it in my bag, and keep on walking, either to the Můstek station or to a bookstore on the square for some warmth.

Is Prague really any colder than Chicago in winter? Perhaps because it's farther from the Equator? Probably not, but somehow it *feels* colder there. The air pierces right through my clothes. I find myself blowing out more little bursts of air as a reaction to the cold. Or, perhaps, as a reaction to my imagination of the cold.

I am also alone there in winter, and because I am alone I'm silent and wandering, and all there is to think about is the state of my mind and my body, which feels like an island there. In winter I'm not talking with a group of friends in the street or on the sidewalk as often. I'm bundled up, and I therefore feel less free to move. I must huddle into comfort. Maybe the ability to move is the reason I'm more okay with visiting the square in the summer than in the winter—lounging when you're an island is an easier thing to do when the air isn't out to get you.

There's a place there called Ouky Douky, and I've gone every day during my winter visit. I first found it when I studied abroad, stumbling onto it when I was exploring the Prague 7 neighborhood on foot and found, just down the hill from the pension I lived in, what looked from the outside like a used bookstore. It's only half a bookstore, though—one room is dedicated to shelves full of Czech books (though one small section holds books in English), and the other room is a café for eating, drinking, smoking.

I like Ouky Douky because it's filled with young people and most of the music they play is in English; it's popular American music I recognize, although some of the artists are British or Swiss or from some other country whose pop music is sung in English. At its base, this place feels like a home inside Prague. It isn't known for harboring burgeoning intellectuals, like the Café Slavia or the Narodní třida (National Theatre), but it's filled with students doing homework and twenty-somethings on dates and groups of young people just smoking and drinking and talking. And it feels good to be around that. I'll read a book while drinking a large beer or order a ham sandwich and play around on the internet. Sometimes I'll use the place to get serious reading or writing done. It's a nice atmosphere to wind down in and a nice place to bring a friend who hasn't seen it before.

Even this place, though, is a falling back on my Americanness. The servers, all young and attractive, speak English, and the menu is half in English, and even some of the clientele speak English, and while this puts me at ease, it feels as if I'm just taking advantage of my American position. I smile lots here, tip better than is customary, and order in Czech when I know how, but I can't help but think every time I walk through the door that the servers are thinking *The American is back again.* I can't help thinking they're a little frustrated with my lack of Czech fluency or my sitting alone (which they might consider loitering), because I don't seem as pleasant to deal with, as a loiterer, as all the people who come in with their friends and lovers. I try not to let my paranoia show. I bring out my politest self when I enter the café, managing to grab a seat under the guise of my being welcome there. I need to have confidence in my ability to feel welcome.

During recent visits to Prague I've thought about the way I've been eating, not just as an omnivore but as someone who often travels alone. Beginning with my omnivorism: like most people, I assume, I'm trying to fill my plate with foods I'll enjoy because I'm no longer being fed by my mother and father and I don't have to worry about what they put on my plate.

I'm looking for something to change, though. Something on principle. Writers like Jonathan Safran Foer (in *Eating Animals*) or Roger Scruton (in "A Carnivore's Credo") don't have me converting to vegetarianism, but they do get me thinking about my diet and how to turn it into one with a higher moral and ethical stance—one where I've considered the treatment of the food by all parties involved and, in effect, the treatment of my body by the food itself. I've given up burgers from fast-food restaurants, for instance, not because I don't enjoy their taste but because I want to believe I'm treating both myself and the cattle involved better by not giving those restaurants my money. I'll be happy to get locally procured beef, or beef from a place that doesn't buy it from some factory farm where cattle are squished together in unimaginable distress. "The onus," Scruton writes, "lies on the carnivore to show that there is a way of incorporating meat into a life that does not shame the human race," and I've been trying, for a while now, to be a little less shameful by way of my diet.

I've been doing this since the first time I studied in Prague, when a classmate told me that, for ideological reasons, he was a vegetarian only in the United States, which I never questioned. Something clicked with me then, and ever since I've looked for clever and inexpensive ways to make myself feel more virtuous about the way I choose my meats. I began eating more seafood. Buying veggie burgers. I tried to stop eating anything on four legs for a while, but failed at this because I like pork. I learned that everything I attempted to quit cold turkey showed me what it was I wanted to keep in my diet.

On days I don't cheat (i.e., when I'm not drunk), I manage to cut my diet to one serving of meat per day. It makes me think, every morning, about which meal I'll want to include meat in and which meat I'll want to eat, and something about this choosiness is exciting. I'm reducing my meat consumption, contributing less to the meat industry, and adhering to a principle—one that sometimes feels an awful lot like riding a high horse.

As I begin to think about my eating habits in Prague, I also begin thinking about how often I eat alone. I know my solitary self very well, and I also know how I act when I'm single: I fall into typical bachelor behavior, knowing I'm the only one I have to look out for. I eat inexpensive foods, cook nothing too fancy for myself, and, overall, I let myself be a far from picky eater.

Maybe this is why I run so often for the sausage in Prague. I think about my taste buds and nothing else, knowing that, because I'm not just single here but also alone, I can neglect thoughts of anything else. Eating is an act that feels so much different when you're alone; you get to think about taste over healthy choice, perhaps not just because you're only looking out for numero uno but because you're trying to quell a sense of loneliness with the tastiness of food and drink.

I've thought too about the way I drink. While I waited until twenty-one to become a drinker, the few years following my birthday were anything but principled: essentially I got drunk on my twenty-second birthday, and I stayed drunk for half a decade. I grossly mistreated my friends and myself. I partied plenty, both with company and alone. I tested myself with science: I now know that my "far gone" points are at eleven beers, *or* two bottles of red wine, *or* sixteen shots. (One night I managed fourteen of vodka and two of whiskey.) I've gotten in arguments that ended in wrestling. I once backed a friend's car out of a parking lot and into a tree. I've fallen asleep on the city bus and woken up in the suburbs. I've fallen halfway into a manhole. I've taken multiple taxis home in the same trip, thinking I was using public transit.

These moments can be funny only because I survived them. But when I look back at them I'm saddled with guilt because of the possibility that any of these things could have gone frightfully wrong.

Now there's no science, and there are no manholes, but I've still tried to be critically reflective about how I drink socially. My social anxiety had me overdrink for years, when I tried very hard to convince myself that more beer, more shots, or more wine would put me at ease, would make me less afraid to be around others. But in truth my anxiety showed me I just wasn't drinking around the *right* others.

I've come to enjoy a Belgian White or two, or a honey whiskey on the rocks after a meal, not just because they're nice digestives but because they make time for slow conversation. I've learned to drink this way in the United States and in Prague, and I'm surprised, in retrospect, by the fact that Prague's cozy pub atmosphere never had its way with me when I was younger and looking for a way to settle into the city.

Beer culture is a source of immense pride for Czechs, my ex-professor Petr explained to me during a visit to his office. He explained that the collectivity of any nation depends in part on having something that they're the best at or can identify with, and for the Czechs, it's beer. He called their beer culture an "ambiguous culture," like America's gun culture, in that "it might ruin some families and so on, but at the same time it has some positive issues." I think that America's gun culture probably disrupts more lives than the Czechs' beer culture, but I agree with him on pride.

Czechs consume about 140 liters of beer per person per year, he told me. But "it's not just drinking," he said. "It's also paintings on the wall in a pub which tells you that drinking beer is the best thing you can do in the world. It's the idea of a pub like your local home. Like something where you receive just positive things, okay? You come for a beer, and they bring you a tasty beer. But the same thing, in contrast to a real home: they never put any unpleasant things or difficult, challenging things in you, and so on. All of these local pubs, they're based on these home-like feelings—that these people sit at the same tables, the same chairs, day after day, and they are recognized by the waiters or waitresses as distinctive, unique individuals. Most of these regular-goers, each of them has a specific mug of a certain shape or a certain sticker attached on the mug, okay? And the waiter brings beer to the person in his or her mug. So you have these domestic-like qualities of these local pubs here, and, as I'm saying, in contrast to a real home, you don't have these negative feelings which exist in real homes."

"What do you mean when you say, 'real home'?" I asked, as if there could be such a thing as a fake home. Homes are constructed, I thought, and therefore always real to the people who build them.

"A pub is kind of pseudo-home, or virtual home," Petr said. "But by 'real home' I mean the real apartment or the house you're living in, and the real family people, and so on. And this pub company is kind of fake family, okay? It's people whose histories and records you know, but in contrast to a real family, you can choose the topics you want to talk about, and so on.

"In a real family, you need to talk all the topics," he said, "even unpleasant topics. You know, lack of money or infidelities or whatever. In a pub company, you're talking just the positive topics, or, if negative topics, it's again this kind of shared opinion, okay, that all people there, say, complain about the politics and all of them agree that politics is a big shit, okay? So it's just this kind of pleasant existence, and that's why, I guess, beer is such a big issue."

I thought about the TV show *Cheers*. I thought about Euro-American kitsch, the kind found in chain cafés like Panera or Barnes and Noble, which have paintings all around showing off people from a beautiful era being beautiful and happy and perfect together. Even the image of this doesn't feel fake, though; it doesn't feel like an unbelievable thing in Prague to see pub families. When I'm there I'm even guilty of frequenting the same pubs and restaurants, where the staff may not know my name but they know my face, and they know what I want to drink because I order it over and over again. I wasn't a regular anywhere when I lived in Chicago, and if I was at a bar alone to stare into space or at a wall, I didn't feel surrounded by family. Even a fake one.

I feel an obligation to build this "pub family" when I'm in Prague; maybe it would help me feel more welcome there. I feel like I should be talking to young strangers about new wonderful films they've seen or upcoming concerts or what the best items on the menu are—anything that isn't inhibited by a barrier of language. And I could build this pub family by using drink, because drink, like food, is often a communal experience, enjoyed in the space of guttural laughter and jovial conversation, and I never do enough there to join in communal experience. I'd be a bit more virtuous if I contributed to a pool of pleasantries established by camaraderie.

There was a young street vendor standing in the cold at a food stand in Staroměstske náměstí, Old Town Square, on a night when I was looking for *klobasa* in a bun. A couple of the stands I'd visited in Vaclavské náměstí were closed for the winter, but their signs mentioned "partner" stands that could be found in other parts of the city center. Perhaps I'd found one here, I thought. So I walked up to the man at the counter, and he grew a smug smile knowing he'd hooked me, the tourist or the student or whoever he thought I was because I was obviously not from around here. The hood on his black and gray winter jacket was tight over the rounds of his face, and when I looked at him I saw both youth and confidence.

He gave me a quick rundown of the menu: he had various sausages, all of which were in plain view on the grill in front of me, as well as desserts and beers in a minifridge and hot plum wine in something that looked like a Crock-Pot. I told him I'd take a *klobasa*, pointed to the one that looked the tastiest and most familiar, and he smiled, nodded, and placed it in a bun, adding my mustard and serving it to me with his big grin. I said thank you, then walked to a semi-heated table near the stand to eat and watch the tourists take pictures in the square, posing in front of buildings and in front of the fountain in the middle, and I remembered how it felt for the square to be that new to me.

The first time I went to Prague, my class had gone to the square, walking from Karlův most to Staroměstske náměstí, to see what I think was a Dalí exhibit. We were shown Prague's Astronomical Clock for the first time, and told about its beauty and precision and the legend behind its maker's eyes being burned out with an iron so that he could never make another. We crossed the square, and though I'm sure there were tourists taking pictures then, all I could do was keep looking back at the clock as I walked, knowing I'd never seen a clock so old in my life.

When I finished my sausage, I went back to the stand for some wine. It was cold out, and I wanted both a buzz and to feel the warmth that came from holding a hot drink in my hand as I walked. Plum wine would do.

The young man asked me what I was doing in Prague. I lied to him. I told him I was studying literature and would leave at the end of spring. I lied because I felt defeated by the smug smile that made it seem like he knew he got me, the American, to pay more for a *klobasa* in Staroměstske náměstí than I would have somewhere else in the city because I didn't know what I was doing there and I'd pay for any novelty I saw. I lied to retaliate against defeat.

It wasn't the young man's victory, I thought. It was mine, because I got my mustard and my wine and *I* tricked him into thinking I was new to this place by approaching him and then saying that, by virtue of studying there, I was better than the people who stood behind me taking pictures, and that I knew he didn't trick me into paying more for my *klobasa*.

But he did win. Because I did pay more. And I did it because I love that damn mustard—that mustard that is always so good and so new to me, new every time I taste it because it's not what's in the States. And because I'm enough of a glutton to take the bait every time.

A GOOD FAKE CZECH

I walked through the Kampa Island neighborhood one day, looking for a spot in the city I'd seen once in a picture captioned "The Venice of Prague." In the picture there was a water wheel along, I assume, the Vltava, in a spot where the river seemed to narrow and one could walk along its banks. Strolling through Kampa I felt one distinct thing: though Praguers and Parisians may disagree with me on this, walking along Kampa felt like walking along the Seine.

I've been told the rent is very high in Kampa, and I began to understand why as I walked along the road. On my left the frigid Vltava flowed behind a brush of thin, bare trees, which I imagine are gorgeous and flourishing in spring and summer, giving the road the serene feeling that comes with a tree-lined river. To my right the buildings stood like blocks with flattened fronts, packed next to one another with all the modernity of a first-class European city.

It didn't feel like *Prague* in Kampa. It felt instead like Prague had tried to abandon itself, copying the architecture of a place like Paris to keep the neighborhood from looking too old, I presume to attract Prague's nouveau riche.

It was strange to look behind me, as I could see Karlův most, the Charles Bridge, knowing that the road at the end of the bridge led to Staroměstské náměstí, Old Town Square, a part of the city trapped in time and unweathered by all that has passed through it. A part of the city that has endured.

Looking forward again, seeing all the flattened fronts made me feel I'd crossed a border somewhere—as though I'd stepped over a line that divided two cities, or even two countries, and had walked into the one people rush to for a taste of Western Europe. That was it, I realized: Kampa reflected the European cities I'd seen that, in the way American suburbs have neighborhoods with identical houses separated by identical yards in a Stepfordesque image of uniformity, have all these flat-façade buildings that provide the same illusion of oneness. A oneness of culture where, even when everything looks different, it looks the same.

What kind of person wants to live in Kampa, I wonder. I've pictured Kampa's demographic as being filled with well-off immigrants (Italian, American, French, etc.) who want something quiet and peaceful, with trees for their children. Trees, at least in my own childhood, symbolized comfort and quiet and play, and in any city I visit now I have trouble equating trees with danger. Though I grew up next to the woods, which harbored many dangers, the trees planted in sequence along a city street in front of a row of houses instead feels homey to me.

Walking down that road in Kampa gave me a sense of displacement—a sense of feeling I'd been thrown out of Prague and into some other place. I've heard Prague has a number of these neighborhoods, neighborhoods built to look like some other city in some other country, and I've always wondered if these neighborhoods make their inhabitants feel as if they've *beat* something, as if they've triumphed against Prague's ever-lingering topographical division of nationalities and classes. Or, perhaps worse, if they feel like they've beat it by becoming a part of it— by joining a system that allows those with money, most of them non-Czech, to build a safety zone that's segregated from the locals.

"What is riskier than living poor in America?" asks MSNBC correspondent Melissa Harris-Perry in a 2012 interview on Martin Gilens's book *Why Americans Hate Welfare*. "Seriously," she says. "What in the world is riskier than being a poor person in America?

I live in a neighborhood where people are shot on my street corner. I live in a neighborhood where people must figure out how to
get their kid into school because maybe it'll be a good school and
maybe it won't. I am sick of the idea that being wealthy is risky.
No, there is a huge safety net that, whenever you fail, will catch
you, and catch you, and catch you. Being poor is what is risky."

I mention this because being in Prague makes me think a
lot about both money and risk, and because I want to dissect
whatever the "safety net" of American status might be. While
being wealthy, or even just well-off, in America might feel safe,
there's still a way to escalate this safety; in my experience and
observation, one can be safer than someone well-off in America
by being well-off in a country that's poorer than America.

It isn't always like this, though. None of my friends or peers
who have left America to live abroad have been *forced* to do so,
but some of them *have* placed themselves in riskier situations
than the ones the United States presented them with. If I stayed
there, if I remained in Prague and decided not to go back home,
I've imagined what I would do to secure myself in a city that
makes things difficult for its nonlocals. I've imagined that, as an
American, I could get a job teaching English, maybe tutoring
on the side. I might try to freelance or get a staff job with the
Prague Post, the local Anglophone newspaper. I could even look
for more Anglophone publications and tell them, "Hey, I'm a
commodity! I know American English, and I'll let you use that
however you want." I'd rely on the fact that I'm a U.S. citizen,
fluent in the linguistic currency of diplomacy.

This is First World guilt, I guess. And it arises from the fact that
while I know I am not middle class in the United States (there's
a tax bracket for measuring this sort of thing), I *am* middle class
in the Czech Republic, and I haven't wanted to look at myself
and say that this is why I've chosen this place. While the novelty
of the parts of Western Europe I've seen has worn off for me, I

keep returning to Prague knowing I have nothing to worry about there as far as money's concerned. I can survive on cheap beer and food and purchase used books at Shakespeare & Sons in Malá Strana, and I feel stupid and annoying knowing I can get away with it. Knowing that, even when I studied there in college, I lived the way I wanted to, while many of the locals were having trouble making ends meet.

I feel stupid and annoying because when I figured out that financial ease was one of the reasons I came back to Prague, it sickened me. I've had friends who moved to Italy or to France or to Germany, countries firmly set in the euro, and I chose to study, twice, in a place where the currency would be traded for zilch were I to bring it back to the United States. This isn't the primary reason I've favored this place, but it has helped, and it's a realization I haven't liked one bit. When my Czech friends complain about the price of beer in pubs or food in restaurants, I feel they're complaining about things that aren't all that expensive. But I have room to feel this way because I'm an American who had enough money to travel abroad in the first place, and although I'm not using my nonnativeness to exploit the inexpensiveness of drinks at bars or fancy desserts, I glare at myself knowing I'm there in part because it's financially easy to be.

I can't live like a king there, but I do enjoy spending three or four U.S. dollars on meals that include beer (which is where most of my money there goes anyway), and I enjoy four dollars feeling like *nothing* to me. I imagine I'd pinch pennies in almost any other European city where I'd try to live, but there's something about the absolute comfort of not counting money in my head at all while I'm in Prague that helps to ease the fact that I'm even more of a minority here than in the United States, and that I'm not fluent in the local language, and that the majority of my friends there have been other American students. And while my Czech friends are very dear to me, they don't help me feel any less lonely when they turn to our server at dinner and order in Czech or yell at a reckless driver in Czech or suggest a very cheap place for us to go out to eat because they can't afford much more than that. My money is my trump card there, and since Prague is the *only* place in the world where I've ever felt power and agency by having money, I've needed to navigate the feelings that having this power give me.

Morgan, an American friend, lives in Vinohrady, a neighborhood in Prague I've never been to. When I search for it on Google I'm shown images of a very clean, almost sterilized part of the city that, like Kampa, looks like it doesn't belong.

At coffee one morning Morgan told me she thinks Vinohrady looks Viennese, that it was once its own city, "a wealthy little city that really wanted to distance itself from Prague in sort of a snobbish way." But she loves the neighborhood. And she loves Prague, in the same ways I do, perhaps for the same reasons I do, and after living in this city for years she still finds novelty and wonder around so many corners.

"One day," she said, "it was probably June or July—I had been working, working, working—and one day I was just, I needed some fresh air, I needed a walk, and when I exit my apartment building I always turn left, and this day I turned right. I went behind my apartment building, and there was Narnia. I mean, it was like walking through the back of the wardrobe. There was this beautiful, sprawling park. And it was sunny, and the leaves, you know, mottled the sidewalk. I mean, it was idyllic. And sort of off to the side is a big rose garden. It's just the most incredible place."

I compared what she told me to the neighborhood in Prague where I've stayed the past two times I've been there, Pohořelec, which is filled with tiny markets and apartment buildings all smushed together, and I got a little jealous. Jealous of all the green I imagined, of the "sprawling park" and the leaves and the rose garden. In all the places in my life that I've built up as homes, I've looked for parks, flattened land with vibrant greens, and enough trees to just want to look *up* sometimes. The short walk from Pohořelec to Hradčany is a walk to a castle, and therefore majestic and privileged in its own way. And the walk to the nearby Petřin Hill is a beautiful hike above a city I love, but I've always been picky about the things I want to see when I look out of my living-room window. I want to see green.

I've become picky because I've tried to carry my hometown, a farm town, with me wherever I go. But I'm also picky because, having lived in a genuine metropolis, I want to feel like I have the right to bring my hometown with me wherever I go—like I've earned a spot somewhere in a neighborhood that doesn't feel like a compromise. I can both have and eat my cake.

This requires the illusion that I've moved through social classes since I've become financially independent. In the way that some people want the nicest car or the nicest TV they can afford, I've always wanted the nicest neighborhood I can afford because I want the illusion of having defeated a system that pushes people into places where they'd prefer not to live. I doubt I've ever made as much money as the people in my Chicago neighborhood who share my aesthetic (or my obsession), but neighborhoods have always been my grand prize, and something diva-like in me has set a standard, no matter what town or city I'm in. Whether in Prague or Chicago, I've coveted the portrait of a spring-like stretch.

A stereotype in Prague holds that all Western immigrants and tourists are well-off, and that Czechs "treat them like people who should have just big money," according to my ex-professor Petr one afternoon, when I visited his office at the university. "While the attitude [toward] Eastern immigrants is that these are people are even much poorer than we are."

It's a stereotype I've seen put into effect by many merchants there. As with any city that harbors tourists, there are parts of Prague where food and souvenirs are more expensive than is logical because tourists come to these places having planned to spend the money they've brought with them.

Petr called it a "financial prejudice," in that the Praguers who aren't up to date think that all people live much better in the West and much worse in the East. "It's too big an oversimplification," he said. "But that's how it works, and, again, it's constructed culturally, because under communism almost no one could travel to the Western countries, so we had no idea about the standards of living in Germany, Britain, or USA, okay? And then, after communism collapsed, some people of course traveled. They could get the picture. They could see that, say, in U.S., it's much more complicated—that you have, I mean, people are truly doing well and riding their Volvos or BMWs. At the same time you have homeless people in the cities of U.S., and you have people who are very poor.

"Such a typical person for local Czechs came from TV serials like *Dallas* or *Beverly Hills* [90210] and *Dynasty*, and so on. It is a big thing in the 1990s, okay? And that's why the Czechs made this kind of simplification that all Americans are like J.R. From *Dallas*. That each one of you has some oil and big money, okay? And some Czechs still have difficulties to understand that, say, you have a U.S. student who comes here but comes just with a backpack and he or she needs to be careful about the budget, and so on."

He calmed a bit, took a second to figure out how to conclude his thought. "It's changing both ways," he said, which had me straighten my spine. "Because on the other hand the most productive tourism these days is, when it comes to Praha, is tourism from Russia, okay? Because you have these rich Russian tourists who come here these days, and there are much more of them coming than people from USA or Britain or whatever. And they spend pretty big amounts of money here, and they show off gladly that they are rich people."

It churned my stomach when I realized I knew what he was talking about. Czech friends my age had complained about this—had complained about the barrage of Matryoshka dolls on display in store windows and T-shirts reading "Praha Drinking Team" or "Czech Me Out" and had said that it was all very stupid. And I wanted to defend the Russians, because without them the Praguers' economy would be poorer, and then they would have only their springs and summers to get their money floating.

Maybe, though, I was trying to defend the Russians because I felt like I was doing the same thing they were. I felt that, though I'm not rich, I do buy kitschy gifts for friends and sometimes pay more than what's necessary for food, and that I've been "helping" the Czechs by being one of those Americans (read: tourists) who can afford to do so. But my biggest conflict with this city has been that I've always wanted to assimilate with it—to be able to say, with confidence, "I'm not a tourist," which has worked when I've been a student there but not when I've just been visiting.

Knowing that I'll never fit in or belong there is, sadly, likely why I've used the power of money just to feel like there's something I can do there with competence. I can *spend* there—and for all the wrong reasons, it's helped me feel like a better visitor, a better student, and a better fake Czech.

CABARET

There'd been a mishap on the way to Prague's Václav Havel Airport, and I missed my flight to Paris. I'd planned to take a weekend trip there, but the bus I was on had to pull over for repairs, and all of the passengers were unloaded and then loaded onto another bus, which didn't make it to the airport in time for me to catch my flight. After a chat with an employee at the airport ticket counter, who offered me a replacement ticket for $390 (there were no refunds or standbys on missed flights), I said no thanks and went back to the city.

My professor had taken our class out to the Café Louvre to celebrate the end of our first study abroad session. I joined them, surprising a few people at dinner and sitting at the end of our very long table. I watched as my classmates arrived one after the other. A few other friends joined us at the Louvre afterward, and we played a round of pool before deciding we should go out on the town. Five of us eventually found our way to a place whose name none of us could discern, but we recognized one word on their sign: *cabaret*. I asked the others if they thought "cabaret" meant the same thing in the Czech Republic that it meant in the States. We were all curious to find out.

We paid a 200 Kč (about $10) cover per person to get in, which included three shots of liquor. When we entered, descending stairs that took us underground, we saw topless waitresses walking around and a small stage front and center, with two poles for whoever wanted to use them to dance. There was a woman in a bikini dancing, who, shortly after we got in, lost her top in a pole maneuver that required her to go upside down. We raised our eyebrows, but no one else seemed the slightest bit surprised. We tried playing it cool—we were five young Americans (four men and a woman) in a Prague underground bar, with a topless dancer holding no one's attention but ours, and we wanted this not to be obvious.

We went to the bar and ordered our shots. I don't know what happened with my other male friends, but I was immediately pounced on. A server in skimpy shorts and a lime-green bikini top approached me, asking if I wanted any special service.

I tried to turn the tables. I asked her about herself as I took my shots, in succession but with careful pacing. She was from Ukraine, had moved to Prague for a better life. She told me she was studying Czech, English, Italian, French, and German, in order to prepare for whatever a future job might ask of her. She was waitressing part-time, with an incredible amount of hope for a better life.

She caressed my crotch after my first or second shot, and, not wanting to make a scene, I let her. She didn't unbutton anything, didn't unzip anything, didn't go underneath anything, but she kept giving me her backstory as she tried to get me hard. She was a little shorter than I, had dirty blonde hair and crooked teeth. Hazel eyes.

I left our conversation after the third shot, then met my friends in an elevated booth across the room; they pointed out to me that there was a back room, where I saw topless servers walking to and fro, carrying trays full of shots and beer. The room was blocked off by no more than a black curtain, which couldn't have done a worse job of keeping our imaginations at bay.

Two waitresses approached our table, one of whom was the woman I'd just left. The other took a seat on my lap, while the Ukrainian took my friend's lap and asked what we were doing in Prague, whether we liked it, et cetera. This new waitress also grazed my crotch with her fingers, as if she'd been trained to do so with customers who seemed new.

"Do you have any specials?" a friend with an empty lap asked.

My waitress left me for a vacant table, then returned with two small menus. The menus weren't for drinks but rather listed special "amenities" the cabaret offered. It was a menu of sex acts, all of which could be performed on or in front of us for a price, though none of them penetrative intercourse. The menu was printed in Czech and English.

"We'll give you full lesby sex show for 500 koruns each," the waitress said, "and the girl gets in free." They offered to take us to the back room and let us watch them sex each other up. We declined, with politeness and embarrassed smiles.

This was my first experience in an adult entertainment venue, and I'm glad I was with friends. When I was in high school, and during the beginning of college, there was a "gentleman's club" about fifteen minutes outside of my hometown that the guys I was in school with liked to brag about visiting after they had turned eighteen, but I never joined them and never went by myself. I could never see the benefit of visiting a strip club, maybe because I thought it made me more of a gentleman *not* to visit one, or maybe I thought that if one could look but not touch, then one might as well watch porn at home instead of spending money on live dancing.

I've walked by many strip clubs in many cities, but their lights have never reeled me in. Minneapolis has a string of pink signs that awed me more than the possibility of live nudity, and living in Chicago for so long I had the opportunity to duck into this club or that one, had I wished to watch someone work for tips in a unique way. In Prague no one is shy about advertising nudity or the idea of sex; sometimes slot machines are advertised as well, letting patrons know they can have a three-in-one night of gambling, alcohol, and breasts: a hedonistic adventure.

I want to digress for a second, to think about a weekend trip I once took to Geneva, Switzerland, when I was in college. There was a night when, on a long walk alone just a few blocks from the hostel I was staying in, I found myself in what one might call Geneva's red-light district, though the lights weren't actually red. I remember violet, and prostitutes in short skirts and dresses pacing the sidewalk waiting for customers. Some were men dressed in drag, but I doubt that in this scene it mattered.

I walked down that street on purpose instead of taking what would've been an easy turn, and I was flirted with by every street worker, some in French and some in English, some with a woman's voice and some with a man's, and I felt a small sense of pride in not turning myself away from them. Instead I walked right past them, as if to let them know I wasn't bothered by what they did but that I still wasn't interested. It felt good to confront, but reject, seedy proposals.

I felt the same sense of pride when I met the waitresses at the cabaret in Prague. Although their offers are appetizing to many men and women, I've never felt a strong enough sense of urgency for sex that I'd want to pay to watch or have it. And being around friends, however willing they might secretly have been to watch a "full lesby sex show," would've made the situation awkward for me.

What grabbed my attention at the cabaret in Prague wasn't that the Ukrainian woman had offered sex or had tried to turn me on, but that she had high hopes of escaping a former life in her homeland. If what she told me was at all true, she was bursting with desperation, learning languages and getting into a line of work where she saw an opportunity for betterment. I couldn't help but wonder who she was, or how dire her situation was, in reality.

Because the waitress was Ukrainian, I thought of her as being part of a very distinct caste in Prague: Many have told me that Ukrainians in Prague are given the jobs none of the locals want, like repairing streets and washing windows. But couldn't it have been more serious? Could she have given herself to the sex industry because she saw no other possibility for "making it" as an immigrant in Prague?

For some reason the first question I had when I left the cabaret wasn't whether or not the women were technically prostitutes but about what kind of venue I'd just visited. Had I now been to my first strip club, or was the cabaret something more? Because the Czech Republic nowhere near resembles America's façade of sexual puritanism, it's possible that no one in Prague would bat a lash at the cabaret's existence because they saw sex work as no big deal; it's also possible, though, that no one would flinch because they accepted the cabaret as a necessary reality for some of Prague's immigrant workers.

If it's at all accurate to say that a growing occupational trend for Czechs is to work in the service industry, capitalizing on Prague's touristic centrism by serving food and drink, is sex in its many forms also a service? To play devil's advocate: Why is serving coffee or beer more acceptable because you do it while wearing your clothes?

"If pornography is a timeless world freed from social responsibilities," Phillip Lopate writes in "Renewing Sodom and Gomorrah," an essay on porn theater, "it is also a static one. The problem it has always faced as entertainment is how to build interest. . . . Even when the entertainment is live, the convention that the performer herself cannot be made love to means that, for all the provocative come-ons of the artiste, the customer must remain as though in a stupor, interpreting but not interacting." Just how close is the resemblance between those who patronize adult entertainment venues and those who enjoy the theater? Aside from the obvious fact that the audience in a strip club or cabaret has both pent-up sexual energy and an elegiac demeanor, in attendance in order to lift up their spirits (rather than because their mood is already high), those seeking live adult entertainment are well aware that they're in an atmosphere requiring interpretation, like watching a play unfold before their eyes. If they're "interpreting but not interacting," though, don't they volunteer themselves for a little letdown, prepared to return to their daily lives after a couple hours of fun?

The stakes are different when one can get oneself off in this theater. If, as the rules state, one can do almost everything but engage in full sex with the actress, is this a way to transform a somber mood into an uplifting opportunity at role-play? Almost no one enters a sex café looking for love in a real sense, but a more superficial love might be found in one's ability and opportunity to play as a sexual partner.

I don't imagine that any of us at the cabaret were the type to have ordered from the sex menu, volunteering ourselves to be taken by a waitress for a solo performance, but I'm going to pretend for a second that I am the type. I don't remember the menu in full, but had I, say, ordered a blow job, I probably would've been pulled behind the black curtain and back into a small room with a booth, then told to sit back and relax. Would this private session have come with any conversation? Any alcohol just to fluff us both? For however long the session lasted, who, in our pretend worlds, would I have been to the waitress, and who would she have been to me? Would I have played the role of her financial knight, saving her from having to report an embarrassing shift? Would she have been the story I tell at all the parties I attend throughout the rest of my twenties?

I'd also be admitting total naïveté if I didn't at least wonder whether those women working in Central European sex cafés, however innocuous the word "café" may be, are victims of sex trafficking or just immigrants trying to work. There might be a cruel pimp behind it all, which would change everything about the possibility of my enjoying any time I'd spend receiving top-less service. Because the Czech Republic is so close to Slovakia, Ukraine, and Russia, which have their own reputations when it comes to the sex trade, shouldn't I at least trouble myself to wonder whether the women I encountered were slaves?

Maybe I'm not worried enough about any of this. Maybe I'm worrying too much. But when looking back on a time when I visited a place unlike any venue I can think of in the States, it seems most responsible of me to consider multiple possibilities about what kind of place I visited. Anything else would be neglectful, and I might find myself in the unfortunate position of having been the ignorant American tourist, a label and identity that I'm always trying to flee.

I've worried about what to call the waitresses at the cabaret, but diction alone doesn't help me grapple with my experience because the cabaret brimmed with possibilities. It was possible for my friends and me to get drunk and have a little foreign fun. It was possible to sit around and enjoy being part of a live, interpreting audience in a pornographic theater, and it was possible that this theater held something horrific behind its curtains.

Like when I walked down that street in Geneva, I may just be helping myself feel respectable about my ability to reject. Spending time in a place like Prague, and encountering a place like the cabaret, has me reposition myself, but in a way that evokes my empathy. I get uncomfortable having been to places like the cabaret or the street in Geneva because the jobs these women hold are very real, and for some, I'm sure, inescapable.

At the end of the night at the cabaret, I went to the bathroom and found that a friend had gotten himself stuck in a stall, yelling and pounding on the door from inside. After telling him I could hear him, I went to find one of the waitresses and asked her how to get him out. She just said, helplessly, "There is no key."

She went to find her manager, but my friend and I ended up breaking down the door, wood and metal flying behind the toilet. We left the bathroom right away and went back to our booth. "We have to go," I told the group; considering we were Americans who had just broken public property in a foreign establishment, leaving seemed like a good idea.

As we walked out, we spoke hurriedly about the adventure we'd just had, saying things like, "That was crazy!" and, "I can't believe that just happened!"—referring both to the stall door and to being in the cabaret in the first place. What we didn't do was talk with any deep thought about the fact that the place even existed or about the nuances of its operation or about how the women ended up there. We were just glad to have found it, glad to have survived it. And, like any good tourists, glad to have endured a crazy night.

AN IDEA OF PRAGUE

I'm revisiting the bar where I celebrated my twenty-second birthday. Bar Barka, in Prague. It's a bit different now. Years ago it had the signature of being a sea-themed bar, designed to look like the deck of a pirate ship; now it's just a bar that sits slightly underground, still decorated with scuba tanks, a deep-sea diving helmet, life rafts scattered about. All remnants of piracy are gone.

The bar's entrance, the way I remember it, used to make me feel like I was approaching a ship head on, all on deck except for the ship's bowsprit. Wood composed the walls and the floor, life rafts were still hung all around, but there were no preserved and petrified stingrays or sea horses or pictures of coral reefs like the ones on the walls now. What I remember was a little sketchier, a place my friends and I were wary of entering the first time we saw this place, worried we'd stick out as young, lost Americans.

From what I can recall of my birthday, I was treated to too many shots of absinthe and vodka. I don't know how I managed (even with help) to get back to the pension, where a classmate and I went to her room to fool around until we were found out and I went to bed.

This bar, these memories—neither especially fond nor especially painful for me to revisit—don't reek of nostalgia. It isn't a place I ever want or need to be in again, but I came back because I thought that I might *feel* the nostalgia, that nostalgia that's supposed to hurt, that holds a bittersweet tinge, the first swallow of whiskey before a luscious aftertaste.

My own memory of this place doesn't fit what I see now, which is gimmicky—too reminiscent of all the themed bars and restaurants in the United States and, because of this, inauthentic in its Europeanness. I don't like it now because it doesn't fit my idea of Europe.

"My idea of Europe": this word choice is historically dangerous, though I hope to circumvent any shivers by noting that my idea is nothing I could, or would, implement by any measure of force. I have no desire to change what I see here. Just to report it.

My idea of Europe begins with being lost—lost at the tongue and at the eyes and at the ears. I've taken Spanish and French in school, but not enough for any real navigation—and being able to navigate language, idiom, and culture helps me feel at home. There's an estrangement in all of this that I feel whenever I'm in Europe.

In Europe I feel five again. When I was five, my oldest sister was taking Spanish and used to label the things around the house with Post-it notes in Spanish vocabulary. *Cama* for bed, *luz* for light, *puerta* for door. In Europe I find myself whispering foreign words again like I did when I was little, often in languages I have little to no understanding of. I'm reading signs and trying to sound out the words as if it'll help me learn the language, though I know it won't. My pronunciation might get a little better, but there's nothing I'll absorb here by whispering.

Not just Europe in general but Prague specifically has over the years become my third home—after Normal and Chicago—because of the things I've learned to navigate there. I've studied there twice, once as an undergraduate and again during graduate school, and I've visited for leisure, but I'm still a stranger there. Still a stranger in my third home. I watch others to try to discern how I, the American, might have offended them. Am I standing too close? Do I take up too much room, like an American manspreader? Did I use the wrong, an *insincere*, thank you? How long of a look counts as a stare?

What am I allowed to do there but shouldn't because I'm still an alien?

My idea of Europe continues into aspects of Prague's architectural makeup. I've always been awed by churches; I even fiddled with architecture and floor plans late in elementary school because I thought that maybe I'd become an architect. I didn't, but I still learned to marvel at the buildings other people could draw, especially churches. Churches have a majesty to them that I don't see in other buildings; perhaps it's because they're spooky in that always-connected-to-the-other-side way, but churches evoke a measure of respect that I just don't have for other buildings.

There's also landscape. There are greens in Europe that don't exist in the United States: pine trees sitting atop large hills in Germany and along the highway in the Czech Republic that I'm not going to find anywhere else, wouldn't want to find anywhere else, that have me envying Europe's rural populations. Suburbs of a city like Chicago are perfect for commerce, sure, but drive twenty minutes outside of Prague or Paris and you'll be met by smiling old women on the sidewalk in aprons wishing you a good day.

This leads me to my final idea of Europe. I've been to Paris, Nice, Cannes, Geneva, Amsterdam, Dublin, and of course Prague, as well as several other towns and villages outside of these main European attractions, if I'm just counting the places where I've covered ground instead of just hiding out in airports, and one of the things that makes Prague and any place east of Germany (though Finland doesn't exactly fit my image of Eastern Europe) appealing to me is their autonomy. I enjoy the pride Central Europeans have in the countries where they live, in their European status—their willingness to own up to the ways they're pitted, financially and otherwise, against places like France and Italy while still raising a beer with joy. So much about Western Europe seems too metro-commercial for me, a quality I've found unattractive.

"If I must describe what Europe means to me as an American," Susan Sontag writes in "The Idea of Europe (One More Elegy),"

"I would start with liberation. Liberation from what passes in America for a culture. The diversity, seriousness, fastidiousness, density of European culture constitute an Archimedean point from which I can, mentally, move the world. I cannot do that from America, from what American culture gives me, as a collection of standards, as a legacy."

What passes for culture in the United States is muddy at best. Though Americans claim to celebrate diversity, there's still a homogenized standard that allows some of us to find ways to pass as good citizens of our country. Those of us who don't pass are left in the margins, visible yet ignored, though still helping America appear as the melting pot it has always claimed to be.

When I was twenty-one, walking down a hallway at school, I passed a bulletin board with a flyer for a study abroad information session for a place called Prague in a country called the Czech Republic. *Not* Czechoslovakia. I attended all of the pre-trip meetings, got to know the students and teachers planning to go abroad, signed up for my classes, and readied myself to leave the United States. What I *didn't* do was learn about the Czechs' language or their history or their culture. The one bit of preparation I did for my trip was read on the internet about whether it would be safe for me to be here as a black person.

I read a lot about Skinheads: Nazis who liked to cause trouble in the streets and who claimed not to be racist but only disliked outsiders. They say things like, "We will get rid of the unadaptables"—drug dealers, homeless people, homosexuals, immigrants, and Roma—because homogeneity is part of what keeps Czech culture "pure." Nazis are among those who've wanted the purity of their nation to be defined by and condensed to history, geography, and lineage.

What I'd come to think was that to be both Czech and a Nazi, modern or not, was to be anti-Czech. During World War II Nazis invaded Prague, sending the city's Czechs into "lesser" parts of the city and deporting its Jews. The Nazis were anti-Czech, anti-Bohemia, anti-mixing. To wish to be a Nazi there is to wish to claim an antiquated, very specific, very narrow German ideal—not to have pride in one's Czechness, which celebrates, perhaps above all, an independent spirit not superior to other nations.

My idea of Prague, and of Europe, is that it should be mixed. Prague is Europe's sixth most-visited city and, I've heard, Europe's most international city per capita. This doesn't mean that when I'm there I'm flooded with the image of other brown people like myself, but this city *is* a hub, a connecting point between, say, western Russians and Italians and the French. So to see a specific group try to oust what composes this city, a demographic of far more than just (white) Czechs is nonsensical at best: a portrait of a group of people whose conservatism is perhaps more bold than their patriotism.

I've seen Nazis in the city exactly once during any of my visits to Prague. There were five or six of them standing near a tram stop one afternoon, all with shaved heads and wearing black pants tucked into combat boots and puffy green jackets. When I saw them, I turned and walked in the opposite direction, frightened, knowing I could maybe outrun but couldn't overpower six of them if it came down to it. A tram came by, and I used it to block their view of me and crossed the street, then turned around and ran my route as I had before, knowing they couldn't see me anymore. I don't know if they got on that tram or not, or whether or not they saw me, but I was safe and have been ever since.

Now I don't even know if they were what I thought they were. I never saw any swastikas; maybe I was presumptuous, reacting to the collective wardrobe of a few individuals, letting anything I'd read or seen or heard about in the news perpetuate the fear that got me running across the street. But *back then* I was terrified. I thought I'd found myself in a scene straight from a movie: a scared young man caught in the open and in plain sight of those who hated him. I saw no choice but flight.

Nazis really aren't prevalent in this city. I'm more or less safe there, and when people ask me if I'm treated strangely or differently because I'm black, I tell them I get stares from locals in their sixties, their seventies, and older, but I'm treated cordially by younger Czechs, those who are less surprised to see a black person walking their streets. I'm greeted, smiled at, nodded at, sometimes said "good day" to, not treated as a local but not treated as unwelcome, either. This is more than I could ask for in some American cities.

"What do you think is the biggest difference between Europe and America?" my Czech friend Katka asked me one night as we sat drinking large beers in the dimly lit mezzanine lounge of the theater where she worked. My first answer to her was language: I said that Americans take *pride* in their English, and that an inability or unwillingness to speak it in the United States sometimes breeds xenophobia, intolerance, and racism. But in Europe, at least in my case, navigating in English seems expected while also feeling wrong. I know I can't learn a new language for every layover I'll have there, but I do expect to speak a little French when I'm in France and to speak a little Czech when I'm in the Czech Republic, though it's presumably all right if I don't. Europeans are willing to accommodate by using their second and third languages, while many Americans want their first one spread everywhere.

There's something more obvious than language in Europe, though. There's heritage. There's nationalism. And I don't mean something political. I mean the difference between an Italian saying, "I'm Italian," and an American saying, "I'm Italian," when their family hasn't set foot in Italy for three generations. Since the United States is so young, not even 250 years old as a nation, this may be why Americans are always reclaiming, or trying to reclaim, our past heritages—to connect ourselves to history and to feel a little less homesick.

Europeans don't have an issue with lost history. They rarely need to retrace their steps, and they have a security in identity that Americans haven't gained yet. Even since the formation of the EU, it isn't as if their borders have melted. The Czechs are still Czechs, and the French are still French.

I once took the most wonderful walk in Prague that I've ever taken there. I decided to revisit my old stomping grounds in Prague 7 near the first place where I lived. I walked from tram station Strossmayerovo náměsti to an uphill street, Janovského, to Umelečka, then past the pension where I stayed at twenty-two. I made my way through a park just down the street from there and decided to try to make my way back to my starting point, before I'd boarded the tram to Prague 7 down at Staroměstska, on foot.

I walked along an empty pathway, children sledding on a hill to my right, passing only a young mother pushing her child in a stroller and an elderly woman walking with her hands held behind her back, as many of Prague's elderly do. Then there was a man, maybe thirty-something, in the park walking his dog.

"Prosím," I said to him. "Anglicky?"

"Just a little bit," he said.

"Uh," I began. "Pendulum?" I motioned with my hand slowly, letting it dangle in the air. I felt stupid not knowing which word they used for what I was looking for.

"I don't know," he said. Then he noticed my hand. "Oh! Metronome!"

"Ano!"

"Uhh," he pointed off to his right. "Čechova," he said. Then, "¿Hablas Español?"

"Un poquito," I said, pinching the air.

"No," he said, a worried look on his face. "Čechova," he continued. "Then, Letenska. And about one kilometer."

"Čechova, to Letenska, then one kilometer," I repeated. "About fifteen minutes?"

"Yes. Maybe."

"Okay," I said. "Děkuju."

"Prosím."

"Čau!"

"Čau."

So I walked. And as I walked down Čechova to Letenska, I passed buildings I'd seen before and thought of how familiar they were to me, how lovely they were because they were visible reminders of my not being in America. A man yelled from his window down to a woman on the sidewalk, while another woman shook a blanket out of her window. The cars parked along the side of the street were miniature. The street signs were in Czech. The buildings ahead weren't made of American glass.

When I reached the park I could see all I'd needed, wanted to see in the distance: Hradčany (the Prague Castle), Petřin Tower, and the Metronome. I'd wanted to see these things because looking at all three at once was a seamless blend of far and recent pasts: where the Metronome now sits once stood the world's tallest statue of Joseph Stalin, which, legend has it, was dismembered and every one of its fragments sent to various parts of the Czech Republic, and then buried so that it may never be reassembled. The castle is a long-standing emblem of Czechness, perhaps the greatest reminder that they were here.

When I looked up at the Metronome and down at the city, at the river, all covered in snow and fog, I saw what I'd loved about Central Europe: endurance. The buildings below have stood there for centuries, but they've been owned, celebrated, and occupied by both the winners and the losers of this city: once-oppressing Germans, clinically stern Russians, ever hopeful Czechs. The

Czechs are still here, and this fact alone has been a reason for my return. I've returned because I've loved them, and I've loved them because they've endured.

"Do we have anything comparable to the Central Europeans' romantic project of a Europe of small nations," Sontag asks, "able to communicate freely with one another and pool their experience, their immense civic maturity and cultural depth, which have been acquired at the cost of so much suffering and privation? For us, who can hop from continent to continent without securing permission from anyone for a night at the opera, could Europe mean anything of that value? Or is the ideal Europe rendered obsolete by our prosperity, our liberty, our selfishness? And the idea itself, for us, spoiled beyond repair?"

I can say that whenever I've come to Europe I haven't wanted to be like the few of my friends who've visited only wanting to see Big Ben and the Coliseum and the Eiffel Tower, all trinkets of a Europe I'm in no hurry to see because it might cheapen my experience. What I've fallen in love with is "the other Europe" (coined by Philip Roth, I believe), a Europe no one back home *romanticizes* because they (a) don't know or care about it or (b) forget it even exists as a part of the continent of Europe. "While all European nations are believed to be a part of a relatively homogeneous cultural and intellectual community," Dina Iordanova writes in *Cinema of the Other Europe*, "the culture of East Central Europe from the second part of the twentieth century has not yet been fully integrated into what is seen to be European." I love this lack of integration; I love that I've never known anyone who wanted to go to Prague just to go shopping, because it means that Prague is still hidden, still protected from all of that American travel gluttony fed by souvenir buyers and picture takers.

This means, I realize, that I have exoticized Prague; it means that I've exoticized this hidden culture and its homogeneity, and that this is what I've been protective of. It's an issue of my loving homogeneity because it isn't something I get much of in the United States, and it therefore becomes foreign and exciting to me.

I've done the same thing with the Czechs that some Czechs have done with the United States. I've come to see their buildings and absorb their customs and learn their vocabulary, but I cannot, will not ever know what it's like to live on their wages or have my thinking be the result of their language or history. A friend of mine, for example, once remarked that 90 Kč was a lot of money for him to spend on a certain food item, and in my head I thought *That's only about five dollars*. Then I felt the shit that comes along with my privileged position of being able to say "only," and I was hit immediately, irredeemably, with an American guilt I never felt in Prague when I was younger. I started to wish for strange, strange reasons that I were poorer.

I wished that I were poorer because I had a wish to assimilate. Which is off-putting to me when I think about it, because the Czechs themselves have spent their entire history fighting assimilation and poverty. For centuries they shared their land with other peoples, not even becoming Czechoslovakia until 1918 and not separating themselves from the Slovaks to become the Czech Republic until 1989, *after* occupation by both the Nazis and the Soviets. Assimilation in the face of oppression, both fiscal and otherwise, has been a method of survival for them, but here I am, treating it luxuriously, abusing the freedom to even be in this country for the sake of donning their clothes. I might be the one ruining my own ideal Europe.

On my last full day in Prague one winter visit, I began my morning by walking from the dorm I was staying in to Petřin Hill. I walked through an entrance with two stone walls, one on each side, like entering an abandoned fortress in the dead of day.

I walked up a small road leading to the top of the hill. When I had studied there the previous summer, my friends and I took a different route. We'd enter from the same gate, see the same stone walls greet us at the entrance, but then we'd make a left at the point where the cobblestones split off into two distinct roads. On this morning I made a right.

The road had been cleared of all snow so that cars, the few that were there, could drive by, meaning the sidewalk was now covered in slush. After all the slush and all the uphill walking I finally saw something familiar: the Petřin Tower. Rumor has it that the tower was built in 1891 to be an exact, miniaturized replica of Paris's Eiffel Tower, which had been built just a couple years before. Rumor has it that the same blueprints were even used for both.

I like the Petřin Tower more. It lights up more beautifully at night, I think, both because it's smaller and less showy and because, looking up from Mala Strana or the Faculty of Arts building at my old university, it's always shown me where home is. Karlův most, the Charles Bridge, is lauded for its spooky yet regal quality, but the next bridge just to the north, Mánesův most, lets me see the tower and the castle in almost perfect synchronicity. Both of my Prague neighborhoods have been behind these two landmarks, and they're what I look forward to seeing when I'm headed back to whatever bed I've learned to sleep in.

When I saw the tower on this morning, I smiled. I walked through a small entrance in the wall to my left, thinking I could make it to the tower from there. But I couldn't. It turned out the way I was headed was closed off, as a man who'd yelled to me from behind had informed me. So I walked around to another entrance, dressed in a black wool coat, leather gloves, and a wool hat I'd bought at a Kmart back in Chicago, feeling a little under-dressed for the morning cold.

I reached the other entrance, and there was a small playground I'd seen once before, on a summer night, now covered in snow. I say "playground" because it looked like a place for children, but there weren't any slides or merry-go-rounds or monkey bars—just a small trampoline maybe four feet in diameter, and a pyramid made of red rope. An adventure to climb, I'm sure.

I walked over to the tower, then thought for a second about going to the top. But it was 9:30 in the morning; the tower tours wouldn't begin until 10:00, and it was too cold outside to stand around and wait. And no one else was around, save for a man who I assumed worked at the tower, dressed like a train conductor and standing outside smoking a cigarette. The little beer stand across the way was closed, and the umbrellas were folded up, frozen to their tables. By the time I'd noticed all of this I realized I didn't care about seeing Prague from its highest point. I'd gotten what I wanted out of the city's winter views almost every other day before this one, and I didn't want to pay for a perspective that was probably prettier in spring and summer. So I walked back to my dorm, this time taking the route I knew, down a winding, slippery trail. Back to a garden next to a monastery overlooking the city, the one place in Prague from which I'd ever seen a sunrise.

There would be no sunrise, though. Aside from its being too late in the day, even if I'd shown up there at five or six in the morning, the haze covering the city would have kept it gray, would have kept me from seeing the kind of clear sky that makes a sunrise worth it. I thought then that maybe I never wanted to return here in winter. That, maybe, I was too used to the comfort of American warmth to let myself really absorb all of this, and that I was too afraid to return there another winter at the risk of ever hating this place.

EPILOGUE

If I wasn't a writer, I could be in love. I could be in love with
something other than writing, perhaps with someone who isn't
a writer, and in a place that isn't filled with people who write. I
could be in a place where no one cares that or what I write, and
neither would I, because I would have built something other
than a book. I would have built a life, a home, a character, maybe
a partnership. I could think about the ways I've grown and the
reasons why I've grown, and try to make sense of what I've grown
into. I've done this with my writing, but I also want to be able
to do this without a single word on paper.

In some settings this is easier to imagine because these places
seem better made for partnership and rest. Some settings are
perfect for finding peace and quiet. Some places, some cities are
built for rowdy youth. I told a friend this once, and he asked for
a list. I gave him Austin, Boston, Los Angeles, Portland. Many of
the suburbs I've seen.

I began thinking about this after once watching an episode of
the TV series *Portlandia*, in which the narrator-protagonist says,
"Portland is where young people go to retire." I saw this episode
years ago while visiting Austin, and I began to think about the
places people go *to retire*. My own retired parents have moved
to the Carolinas, to be with their grandchildren. But they aren't
young people trying to settle. I see young people trying to settle in
many places I visit; they're trying not to move around anymore,
in hopes of being anchored by what they love.

I have been no different. And as I've gotten older I've seen
that I've failed at settling. My trip to Austin in particular showed

me the near-ubiquity of settling and the way certain cities seem better for it than others. Austin seemed to me to have a romantic openness: for walking in pairs, for biking in pairs, for driving to brunch or to dinner or to the movies or to each other's houses. Austin had warmth, perfect for those tired of winter and who find the city ideal for being outdoors, for being in shorts during a live concert or on the way to a bar or during a hike in the city's vibrant gardens. The city invited those filled with hope—hope for success at a new job or for a love life or for the domestication of the self, or perhaps all three at once. Being in Austin, having a nice job, falling in love, and getting a dog seemed like a dream, and one far distant from thoughts of middle age and retirement. That city, like many that feel built for those around my age, sent a warm invitation to ambition and hopefulness.

I went to Austin for a woman. I gave myself a few days to express my love, with the hope that she would understand. She said to me there once, on our drive to dinner, that she just wanted a job with health insurance and a retirement plan, and that maybe this desire meant she's getting old. I didn't think so. I thought it was a normal thing to want to be able to retire someday, to feel secure in one's healthy, rested future. This isn't something I've thought about much for myself, though; I haven't thought about the end of my working days because I don't even know what they would mean for me as a teacher or as a writer—but also because, for now, I just want to keep pushing through. I want to keep trying at things. To keep stretching myself thin, as I'm wont to do, as I do the work I love and enjoy. I haven't thought at all, yet, about how or when I'll stop.

I went to see this woman because she didn't come to me when I asked her if she wanted to; she feared that a visit to Chicago (where I lived then) would come with expectation, and because of this she never budged. I went because I wanted to settle things, because I wanted us to talk things through: cards on the table, hopes and fears expressed, nothing important left unsaid. There was hope here rather than expectation; hope for the full perception of my expressed love. I had hoped that she'd feel flattered, comforted, and warm. Had hoped that, like me, she'd be hopeful.

Years ago, while I was at a conference in Iowa, over the phone she told me she was thinking of moving to Los Angeles. My first thought in response was *We are never going to be together, are we?*, which I didn't say out loud and which made me sink when I thought it. I had hoped, since we'd first come apart, for some mutual place that neither of us would want to leave and that we would love, that we wouldn't leave it not just because of each other but because our work would keep us there.

I want to be in a place where I can work with all my heart and where I can work for a very long time. This, to me, is settling: finding a place to seat myself where I won't feel restless or antsy, but where I'll still feel determined. Determined to work, play, and love and determined to do these things for as long as I'm able. And I must believe that, with enough patience, I *can* find a way to settle. The notion of settling has become more important to me than rest, and it has become as much about geography as it has been about finding love. And I want, I know for certain, to settle.

When I studied psychology during my first years as an undergraduate I really liked learning about Erik Erikson, who theorized about stages of psychosocial development. Sometimes we find ourselves between, rather than within, these stages—a foot in one and a foot in the other, just trying to figure it all out. I felt, through most of my twenties, caught between what he called *Intimacy versus Isolation* and *Generativity versus Stagnation*, meaning I've wanted to be productive both in work and in love. Now, in my early thirties, I want both a solid work ethic and a place that feels like home to me—I want to work (i.e., to teach), to talk about work, to think about work, and not to do it alone.

Having been abroad somewhat often I've made myself practice living with different, and fewer, things than I'm accustomed to in the United States. Unlike, say, a decade ago, I no longer feel I need my own lawn to mow or a car on which I can place my creative bumper stickers. I surely no longer feel a need for a house, which not only would be attached to a mortgage but might also keep me in place for ten or so years.

There's also a question of my own identity within all this pick-and-choose. There's the question of what kind of demographic I hope to surround myself with when I find my ideal home. Would it be, as has been the case with my parents for quite some time now, in a predominantly white neighborhood wherein the façades of every house show off promise and security? Would it be like my neighborhoods in Chicago, green but congested with apartment complex after complex and with neighbors too numerous to count?

And if I am still alone, will it mean finding a neighborhood where it is easy to remain alone (if it's what I want), or will I be surrounded by newly proud parents and their strollers, thereby pressured to create my own rendition of this portrait? As someone who has been predominantly heteroromantic throughout his life, will I even seek out the possibility of being my child's second dad?

So many my age feel lost about what we want to do. So many of us feel underpaid and overworked, just trying to keep our heads above water. And so many of us are confused about where and with whom we belong. We have struggled to know when what we're doing matters to others. I've felt both myself and my friends avoiding, with our work, a heavy, stagnant frivolity.

The thing is that I've wanted to be older and done with movement. Part of this is due to actual relocation: during my eight years in Chicago I had nine apartments, and I eventually reached a point where I wanted to stop signing new leases, a move away from restlessness. I know this was my own fault and that I'd been signing leases because I stupidly picked places to inhabit rather than forge, when instead I should have found places where I wasn't afraid to decorate, wasn't afraid to fall asleep outside my bedroom, wasn't afraid, because of drab kitchens, to make breakfast after someone spent the night. The other part is that I've wanted to feel as though I've navigated *toward* something. Like I haven't been lost or even felt wanderlust, but instead that I've wanted to feel I've had a destination in mind—somewhere green, without lingering overcast days or buildings so tall I crane my neck—and this destination is what I'll get to call home. What I want is an environment that feels like I've forged it, a place that feels like it's been built.

Youth: full of energy and that autonomy often mistaken for cleverness. In youth we often find ourselves stretching, molding ourselves to reflect our passions and enthusiasm. We work toward the shape of a life built from fervor—from love, resolve, myopia. Youth is, after all, about trying to prove one's ability, and we have our late nights, our drinking, and our bodily tricks as evidence. *Look at what I can do*, we say as we peacock.

As we grow, our resolve becomes pointed toward what we want as a *vocation*. If youth is about experimenting in play, then adulthood experiments in work, and with any luck it's work with which we can be in love. This doesn't mean that adults must *always* work but that when they work they should do so with care and in ways that reflect what they love about the world. The adults I've admired, the adults I've loved, have been special to me because of how they've chosen to work: in a way that displays happiness as their wealth.

"A vocation," Natalia Ginzburg writes, "is man's one true wealth and salvation." This vocation, this thing-dedicated-to, is what I suppose I've been looking for all along. But it has been more about commitment than career, more about dedication and a running-toward that I've been striving for as I've gotten deeper into the things I've now been doing for years—deeper into teaching, deeper into scholarship, deeper into my writing practice—and this depth has meant a greater risk of never coming back. A brick tied to the ankle at the bottom of a pool. A room cut off by door after door.

A *vocation*, as Ginzburg defines it, is "an ardent and exclusive passion for something . . . the consciousness of being able to do something better than others, and being able to love this thing more than anything else." I've wandered into the vocation of trying, and I've wished to be better at it than anyone I know. It's shameful and selfish, but I've tried to become someone my friends will miss when I'm not around. It's *selfish* because it isn't exactly generous when I look at what I've wanted to build within and around myself and what I find is usually someone who'll be missed because of his efforts. Although not a "champion," I've wanted to be someone who still gave, who tried hard, and who loved.

I am not a champion—of any kind. I'm not a champion for women, nor for queers, nor for racial or religious minorities, nor for anyone still fighting to be heard. I have strived for improvement with a focus on myself centrally. And I can only hope, if anyone is watching, that my efforts can aid them as much as they've helped me. But make no mistake, reader: I am no hero, and I regret that my vocational efforts have settled so far from sainthood.

The word "settle" is tricky, because while it might imply "settling down" or perhaps "settling for less," what I want it to mean is that I want things to solidify—for my life, my environment, my identity—to settle like clay, from some ambiguous beginning that takes shape and form over time. I want to recognize the shape of a life as it has been formed by my choices, whether or not these choices have been solitary. I didn't visit Austin, for example, because I felt too solitary. I visited to find another sculptor, to let her know that I wanted to find a shape. I've wanted a full sculpture, and I've wanted to watch the process of molding.

Perhaps I've been thinking about settling because my parents have gone into retirement. The idea of retiring, of sitting still, scares me, if only because I can't imagine what I would do without a vocation. My father now golfs; my mother beautifies the lawn; and together they visit amusement parks and dine out and watch sports and go bowling.

What's significant to me about my anxiety is a palpable discomfort with my own movement coming to a halt. Even if I can manage to keep an apartment (or one day a house), I know that I want to stay busy and keep trying, to hold onto productivity for as long as I can. I fear my relaxation turning into laziness.

I'm afraid of the kind of ending that comes with retirement— I'm afraid of this kind of wrapping up of a life, where struggle has met its end at the beginning of leisure. I'm afraid because I have always been struggling, have always been swimming against the density of water, and I fear that if I ever stopped swimming I would drown. Swimming has taught me how to map out so much, and this is likely why I've appreciated the struggle.

"Everything I do, I do because I know I am dying," a professor of mine once wrote. "As we get older," she continues, "we have more to think about in less time—we must think of more in a compressed amount of time." While everything *I* now do, I do because I've felt my own time become compressed, it has also been in an effort to become a less shitty and messy person as I age. And because in aging I've noticed time become compressed in a way I've never been able to perceive before. I've felt myself become able to reflect in a way I've never done before, where I can see with clarity all the swift turns and brushings-against and the things that have helped to mold me. Here, in this looking back, is the way I've made sense of a sculpture—the crafting and carving so intensely noticed, with such an intense gaze thrust upon it, that I can't help but regard every fault.

WORKS CITED

Anderson, Linda. "Autobiography and Personal Criticism." *A History of Feminist Literary Criticism*, edited by Gill Plain and Susan Sellers. Cambridge University Press, 2012, pp. 138–53. Print.

Baldwin, James. *Notes of a Native Son*. Beacon, 1984. Print.

Barthes, Roland. *A Lover's Discourse: Fragments*. Translated by Richard Howard. Hill and Wang, 2010. Print.

Beverly Hills, 90210. Created by Darren Star. Fox. 4 Oct. 1990.

Bílek, Petr. Personal interview. 21 Jan. 2013.

Bílková, Katka. Personal interview. 21 Jan. 2013.

Biss, Eula. *Notes from No Man's Land: American Essays*. Graywolf, 2009. Print.

Bissinger, H. G. *Friday Night Lights: A Town, a Team, and a Dream*. Da Capo, 2000. Print.

Childs, Morgan. Personal interview. 24 Jan. 2013.

City Hall. Directed by Harold Becker, performances by Al Pacino, John Cusack, and Bridget Fonda. Castle Rock Entertainment, 1996. DVD.

Dallas. Created by David Jacobs. CBS. 2 Apr. 1978.

Didion, Joan. *Slouching towards Bethlehem*. Farrar, Straus and Giroux, 2008. Print.

Dynasty. Created by Esther Shapiro and Richard Alan Shapiro. ABC. 12 Jan. 1981.

Full House. Created by Jeff Franklin et al. ABC. 22 Sept. 1987.

Ginzburg, Natalia. *The Little Virtues*. Arcade, 1989. Print.

Growing Pains. Created by Neal Marlens. ABC. 24 Sept. 1985.

Harris-Perry, Melissa. "Book Discussion: *Why Americans Hate Welfare*." Interview. MSNBC. 1 Sept. 2012. Web.

Hauser, Alisa. "Traveling 'Gutter Punk' Homeless Back in City." *DNAinfo Chicago*. 21 May 2013. Web.

Iordanova, Dina. *Cinema of the Other Europe: The Industry and Artistry of East Central European Film*. Wallflower, 2003. Print.

Kundera, Milan. *The Book of Laughter and Forgetting*. Translated by
Michael Henry Heim. Harper Perennial, 1980.

———. *Ignorance: A Novel*. Translated by Linda Asher. Harper Perennial, 2003.

———. *The Unbearable Lightness of Being*. Translated by Michael Henry Heim. Deluxe edition. Harper Perennial, 2009.

Lacan, Jacques. *Feminine Sexuality: Jacques Lacan and the École Freudienne*. Edited by Juliet Mitchell and Jacqueline Rose. Translated by Jacqueline Rose. Norton, 1985. Print.

Lazar, David. *Occasional Desire: Essays*. University of Nebraska Press, 2013. Print.

Les poupées russes. Directed by Cédric Klapisch, performances by Roman Duris, Kelly Reilly, and Audrey Tautou. StudioCanal, 2005. DVD.

Lopate, Phillip. *Portrait inside My Head: Essays*. Simon & Schuster, 2014. Print.

———. *Portrait of My Body*. Anchor/Doubleday, 1997. Print.

Lowry, Lois. *Number the Stars*. Bantam Doubleday, 1989. Print.

Mairs, Nancy. *Voice Lessons: On Becoming a (Woman) Writer*. Beacon, 1994. Print.

The Mickey Mouse Club. Created by Hal Adelquist and Walt Disney. ABC. 3 Oct. 1955.

Morris, Wesley. "The Rise of the NBA Nerd." *Grantland*. 13 Dec. 2011. Web.

My Own Private Idaho. Directed by Gus Van Sant, performances by River Phoenix and Keanu Reeves. New Line Cinema, 1991. DVD.

Portlandia. Created by Carrie Brownstein et al. IFC. 21 Jan. 2011.

Romeo + Juliet. Directed by Baz Luhrmann, performances by Leonardo DiCaprio and Claire Danes. Twentieth Century Fox, 1996. DVD.

Safran Foer, Jonathan. *Eating Animals*. Bay Back Books, 2010. Print.

Sante, Luc. *Kill All Your Darlings: Pieces 1990–2005*. Yeti, 2007. Print.

Scruton, Roger. "A Carnivore's Credo." *The Best American Essays: Sixth College Edition*, edited by Robert Atwan. CL-Wadsworth, 2011, pp. 393–400. Print.

Sontag, Susan. *Where the Stress Falls: Essays*. Picador USA/Farrar, Straus and Giroux, 2002. Print.

Stabile, Carol A. "'Sweetheart, This Ain't Gender Studies': Sexism and Superheroes." *Communication and Critical/Cultural Studies*, vol. 6, no. 1, 2009, pp. 86–92. Print.

Tom and Jerry. Created by William Hanna and Joseph Barbera. 1940.

Total Eclipse. Directed by Agnieszka Holland, performances by Leonardo DiCaprio and David Thewlis. FIT Productions, 1995. DVD.

Trimble, John R. *Writing with Style: Conversations on the Art of Writing*. 3rd edition. Prentice Hall, 2010. Print.

Watch My Feet. Directed by John Bresland, performance by John Bresland. Vimeo, 6 Dec. 2010. Web.

Weinberg, Zoe A. Y. "Raceless Like Me." *Harvard Crimson*. 13 Oct. 2011. Web.

Bigger than Life: A Murder,
a Memoir
by Dinah Lenney

What Becomes You
by Aaron Raz Link
and Hilda Raz

Queen of the Fall: A Memoir
of Girls and Goddesses
by Sonja Livingston

Such a Life
by Lee Martin

Turning Bones
by Lee Martin

In Rooms of Memory: Essays
by Hilary Masters

Island in the City: A Memoir
by Micah McCrary

Between Panic and Desire
by Dinty W. Moore

Sleep in Me
by Jon Pineda

The Solace of Stones: Finding
a Way through Wilderness
by Julie Riddle

Works Cited: An Alphabetical
Odyssey of Mayhem and
Misbehavior
by Brandon R. Schrand

Thoughts from a
Queen-Sized Bed
by Mimi Schwartz

My Ruby Slippers:
The Road Back to Kansas
by Tracy Seeley

The Fortune Teller's Kiss
by Brenda Serotte

Gang of One: Memoirs
of a Red Guard
by Fan Shen

Just Breathe Normally
by Peggy Shumaker

Scraping By in the Big Eighties
by Natalia Rachel Singer

In the Shadow of Memory
by Floyd Skloot

Secret Frequencies:
A New York Education
by John Skoyles

The Days Are Gods
by Liz Stephens

Phantom Limb
by Janet Sternburg

When We Were Ghouls:
A Memoir of Ghost Stories
by Amy E. Wallen

Yellowstone Autumn:
A Season of Discovery in a
Wondrous Land
by W. D. Wetherell

To order or obtain more information on these or other University of Nebraska Press titles, visit nebraskapress.unl.edu.

CPSIA information can be obtained
at www.ICGtesting.com
Printed in the USA
LVHW09s2033310818
588759LV00002BA/194/P